MODERN NATIONALS
THE AINTREE SPECTACULAR

Jockey Richard Guest is all smiles on Red Marauder during the traditional pre-race parade in 2001.

MODERN NATIONALS
THE AINTREE SPECTACULAR

STEWART PETERS

TEMPUS

Tempus Publishing Limited
The Mill, Brimscombe Port,
Stroud, Gloucestershire, GL5 2QG

ISBN 0 7524 2401 7

Typesetting and origination by
Tempus Publishing Limited
Printed in Great Britain by
Midway Colour Print, Wiltshire

Cover photograph credit: John Grossick.

Aintree regular Brave Highlander clears the fallen Edmond at The Chair in the mudbath of 2001. Next to him, jockey Shay Barry clears the obstacle unconventionally, having been sent flying from his mount Moondigua.

FOREWORD

The Grand National at Aintree racecourse has long held a special place in my heart. Ever since my debut as a jockey in the great event, aboard a nine-year-old outsider named Siracusa, it was always a burning ambition of mine to one day reach the winner's enclosure in the world's most famous steeplechase.

As a jockey, I had many memorable adventures in the race, including an exhilarating ride on Bassnet, who was fifth in 1969, and also when Assad showed up prominently for a long way in my final attempt in 1970. But I suppose the closest I got to National glory in the saddle was in 1967, riding the big-race favourite Honey End. The horse, trained by Ryan Price, was in tremendous form coming in to the race, and was made the market leader on the day at 15/2. We were travelling very nicely and had just jumped Becher's Brook for the second time until possibly the most famous event in Grand National history occurred at the twenty-third fence. A riderless horse named Popham Down ran in front of the fence, causing a huge pile-up in which most of the field were stopped in their tracks. After putting Honey End to the same fence a number of times, we finally got over the obstacle, but 100/1 outsider Foinavon, the one horse to avoid the mayhem, had flown, and the rest of us were fighting an uphill battle to try and catch him. Although Honey End ran his heart out to try and reel in Foinavon, it was simply too much to ask, and we eventually came home second.

As a trainer, I feel it is safe to say the National touched my heart, along with the rest of the nation's, on an April afternoon in 1981 when Aldaniti, a horse that I trained and that had suffered unbelievable injury problems, completed a fairytale win under jockey Bob Champion, a man who had successfully battled cancer and had dreamt during his long struggle, of obtaining such glory. Any Grand National winner is undeniably worthy, but that truly was a special day, one that will forever be remembered.

Since then, my Aintree interest has been as strong as ever, and in 1987 with You're Welcome and in very recent Nationals with Brave Highlander, I had one or two moments where I thought victory was on the cards again.

But the Grand National in my mind remains the ultimate test in the jump-racing calendar, an event that holds no comparisons throughout the sport. The sheer atmosphere and excitement generated at Aintree is something to behold. In this book covering the race's modern history, Stewart Peters captures the spirit and passion that is the National and wonderfully chronicles the events of each year to provide a hugely satisfying record of the glorious spectacle that makes the Grand National a race like no other.

Josh Gifford

MAP OF THE COURSE

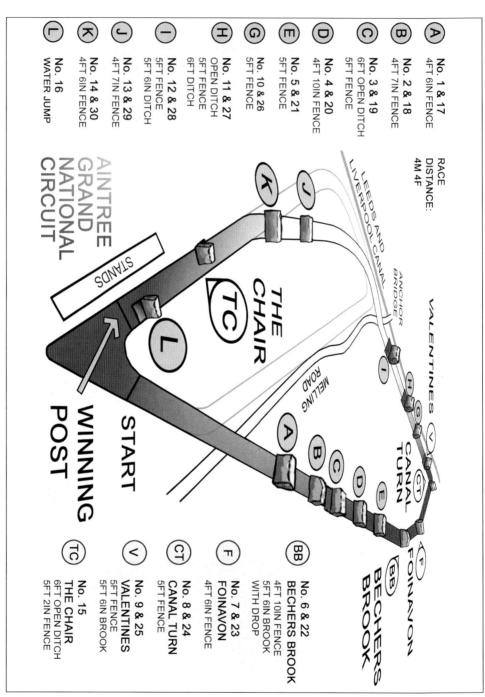

RACE
DISTANCE:
4M 4F

(A) No. 1 & 17
4FT 6IN FENCE

(B) No. 2 & 18
4FT 7IN FENCE

(C) No. 3 & 19
6FT OPEN DITCH
5FT FENCE

(D) No. 4 & 20
4FT 10IN FENCE

(E) No. 5 & 21
5FT FENCE

(G) No. 10 & 26
5FT FENCE

(H) No. 11 & 27
OPEN DITCH
5FT FENCE
6FT DITCH

(I) No. 12 & 28
5FT FENCE
5FT 6IN DITCH

(J) No. 13 & 29
4FT 7IN FENCE

(K) No. 14 & 30
4FT 6IN FENCE

(L) No. 16
WATER JUMP

(BB) No. 6 & 22
BECHERS BROOK
4FT 10IN FENCE
5FT 6IN BROOK
WITH DROP

(F) No. 7 & 23
FOINAVON
4FT 6IN FENCE

(CT) No. 8 & 24
CANAL TURN
5FT FENCE

(V) No. 9 & 25
VALENTINES
5FT FENCE
5FT 6IN BROOK

(TC) No. 15
THE CHAIR
6FT OPEN DITCH
5FT 2IN FENCE

AINTREE
GRAND
NATIONAL
CIRCUIT

STANDS

THE
CHAIR

TC

START

WINNING
POST

MELLING
ROAD

LEEDS AND
LIVERPOOL CANAL

ANCHOR
BRIDGE

VALENTINES

CANAL
TURN

FOINAVON

BECHERS
BROOK

Map credit: Richard Swarbrick.

INTRODUCTION

Ever since the very first running of the Grand National, then known as the Grand Liverpool Steeplechase, back in 1839, this magnificent and unique sporting occasion has provided enthralling stories and races of gripping excitement, year after year. It was a horse named Lottery that won the initial event, and now, with the race extending into its third century of competition, the Grand National is firmly positioned as the most colourful and popular horse race of the year and one of the most important and prestigious events in the entire sporting calendar.

Past runnings of the Grand National have presented glorious and unforgettable chapters in racing history: Gregalach emerging victorious from a record field of sixty-six in 1929, Golden Miller achieving a fabulous double of the Cheltenham Gold Cup and Grand National in the same year (1934) – which no horse has emulated since, ESB taking advantage of the brutally unlucky slip of the Queen Mother's horse, Devon Loch, in the closing stages of the 1956 race, and when the complete outsider Foinavon avoided carnage at the twenty-third fence in 1967 to sensationally win at 100/1.

The modern era of the Grand National has seen the race rise to new levels of sporting excellence and worldwide stature. Passing through uncertain times in the 1970s, when the race's future was clouded in doubt, the National's status was finally secured in the early '80s through the sponsorship of whisky firm Seagram. Currently

Foinavon avoided mayhem at the twenty-third fence to come home a shock winner in 1967.

Although altered in recent times, the big Aintree fences still provide the ultimate test.

sponsored by subsidiary product Martell, the Grand National boasts substantial and ever-increasing prize money, confirming the rich well-being of this legendary event.

Aintree racecourse itself has seen considerable changes in its modern history, with significant reconstruction to the grandstand and general complex making it one of the finest racing venues in the land. On the course itself, the fences have been modified in recent times, offering a truer and safer test of skill for horse and rider. Even so, famous fences such as Becher's Brook, the Canal Turn, Valentine's Brook and the Chair, all ensure that any Grand National victory must be well and truly earned.

Of course, the most important and intricate part of any Grand National are the competitors, and the modern era of the race has seen a tremendous number of brave horses and masterful jockeys combine to give each and every race a perfect mix of romantic sentiment and exhilarating drama. In recent years, there have been many horses that have stood out for their excellence and courage in capturing the great race: the incomparable Red Rum jumped 150 monstrous Aintree fences without error on the way to his record three victories in the 1970s; West Tip, after a fall in 1985, came back for the next five years to establish himself as one of the modern greats; while others such as Aldaniti, Corbiere and Bobbyjo all had a fairytale story behind their triumph. Then there are the 'nearly horses', those that gave their all but ultimately went unrewarded, such as the gallant Crisp, who was only overtaken in the dying strides in 1973 having led all the way, and others like Greasepaint and Durham Edition that turned up year after year for the National to be agonisingly denied victory on numerous occasions. Jockeys like Brian Fletcher, Neale Doughty and Richard Dunwoody have proved masters at conquering the famous thirty fences that Aintree presents, while certain riders found the one-off challenge of the National destined to provide them with constant frustration: such as Jonjo O'Neill, one of the all-time greats of jump racing who endured a miserable time in this event, and Chris Grant, desperately unlucky to finish runner-up three times.

In recent times, the Grand National has featured spectacular races with combative contestants, breathtaking finishes, crushing falls, jubilation, desolation, heartache and hope. As the race continues in to the twenty-first century with its popularity and status as strong as ever, it is hoped that the races that lie in wait in the future bring a blend of as many fascinating qualities as those that make up its modern history.

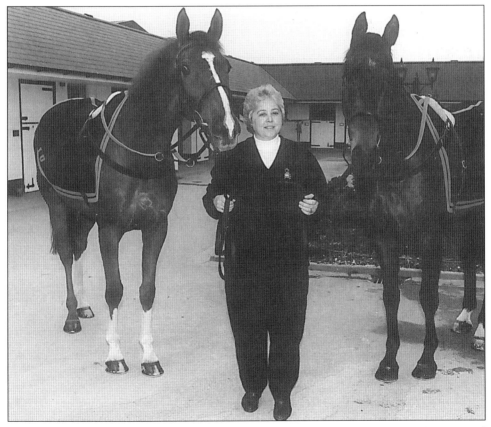

The 'First Lady of Aintree', Jenny Pitman, pictured here with two of her Grand National heroes, Royal Athlete and Garrison Savannah.

1970
GAY TRIP

The Grand National had been used to assembling fields in excess of forty runners during the previous decade, and was only four years removed from seeing forty-seven thrill the crowds. However, the 1970 edition featured the lowest number of runners for ten years, with just twenty-eight facing the starter.

There was, nevertheless, a good influx of quality for this race, with Fred Rimell's eight-year old Gay Trip at the top of the handicap. Owned by Mr Tony Chambers, the horse was recognised for winning his races at two-and-a-half miles, and had captured the Mackeson Gold Cup earlier in the season, while also running a solid preparation for Aintree in the recent Cheltenham Gold Cup.

It had not all been smooth sailing for Gay Trip though, as he came to take his place in the big race line-up. He had been badly injured in the 1968 Mackeson and was off the course for twelve months before claiming the same race earlier in the season. Furthermore, the horse's regular jockey, Terry Biddlecombe, would be missing from Aintree through injury. His place was taken by forty-year-old Pat Taafe, a man who had won the race fifteen years ago on Quare Times.

Fred Rimell's powerful 1970 challenge was bolstered by the presence of French Excuse. The same age as Gay Trip, the horse had been a leading contender for the Grand National ever since winning the Welsh equivalent, and he was the more fancied of the pair, occupying second place in the betting at 100/8. The concern over French Excuse seemed to be the going. The horse's best form was in testing conditions, while at Aintree it was officially good.

It was Two Springs who would carry the mantle of favourite following a consistent season. A win at Chepstow in December was followed by solid runs at Haydock and Uttoxeter. He went in to battle at a price of 13/2.

Red Alligator was now running in his fourth National. The winner in 1968 and third in the chaotic Foinavon race a year earlier, the horse had fallen in the previous year's contest. However, the eleven-year-old had impressed during the season with three wins and three places, and Brian Fletcher's mount was certainly not unconsidered for a second victory.

Two horses listed at 22/1 were trained by Bob Turnell. Bowjeeno had won his last outing while Rondetto was an Aintree regular, who at fourteen was now running in his fifth Grand National. The horse had been well fancied for the race on many occasions, and last year had put in his best effort yet when finishing third to Highland Wedding.

Josh Gifford, who could consider himself unlucky not to have won the 1967 race on Honey End, was looking to end his career as a jockey in the race with victory on 28/1 shot Assad. Gifford was set to start a new challenge as a trainer.

Indeed, once the race was underway, it was Gifford on Assad who led to the first fence, together with Two Springs and the Irish raiders Miss Hunter and Vulture.

Despite the relatively small field, Perry Hill and Queen's Guide both departed from the contest at the opening obstacle.

The first fence was merely an appetiser for the devastation to hit the field at the first big ditch, the third fence. No fewer than eight horses were put out of the contest here, including the favourite, Two Springs, and the veteran Rondetto. Tragically, outsider Racoon fell fatally, breaking his neck.

There was, however, no respite in the action and French Excuse saw his Aintree dreams evaporate after exiting at the Canal Turn, and he was followed out by Bowjeeno, who departed at the tenth, and Red Alligator a fence later. Miss Hunter and Assad were still out in front at the Chair, but by now there were only thirteen runners left in the contest as they went out for the second circuit.

Going down to Becher's Brook for the second time, it was Villay, ridden by his owner Mr Derek Scott, that led. The 100/1 chance jumped the fence first, with Gay Trip going imperiously well on his outside. Behind them came more grief as The Otter crashed out – bringing down Specify in the process. It was particularly hard luck on Specify who had been jumping strongly and, according to his jockey John Cook, had been going as well as anything. The same fence saw The Fossa and No Justice refuse, and this left a band of eight to fight out the remainder of the contest.

Villay still led jumping Valentine's, followed by Miss Hunter, Vulture, Gay Trip, Dozo, Ginger Nut, Assad and finally Pride of Kentucky. They were grouped close enough together to suggest that any of the eight could win, but at this stage, Vulture, Dozo and, in particular, Gay Trip, appeared to be travelling best.

Going to two out, the field had lost Villay and it was now Gay Trip who jumped to the front. Behind him, Vulture was under pressure and Dozo was beginning to get very tired.

Gay Trip, displaying the class of a top weight, was sent clear at the last by Taafe, and keeping on strongly past the elbow, he went on to win very comfortably by twenty lengths. Vulture followed him home and the Irish also filled third spot with Miss Hunter. Having been second at the last, Dozo finished an exhausted animal in fourth place. A quarter of the field had completed, with Josh Gifford ending his Grand National rides in last place on Assad.

It would be Pat Taafe's final attempt at the race and he could not have wished for a better ride than the one the excellent Gay Trip gave him. Despite pitching on landing at the first, Taafe reported a perfect round to give him his second National success.

Fred Rimell could now celebrate his third race victory as a trainer, having previously won the Aintree marathon with ESB and Nicolaus Silver, while for Gay Trip's sire, Vulgan, National glory was also no stranger, having been responsible for former winners Team Spirit and Foinavon.

HORSE/FATE	AGE/WEIGHT	JOCKEY	ODDS
1st **GAY TRIP**	**8.11-5**	**P. TAAFE**	**15/1**
2nd **VULTURE**	**8.10-0**	**S. BARKER**	**15/1**
3rd **MISS HUNTER**	**9.10-0**	**F. SHORTT**	**33/1**
4th **DOZO**	**9.10-4**	**E.P. HARTY**	**100/8**
5th Ginger Nut	8.10-0	J. Bourke	28/1
6th Pride Of Kentucky	8.10-0	J. Buckingham	13/1
7th Assad	10.10-1	J. Gifford	28/1
Bowgeeno - *Fell*	10.10-13	J. Haine	22/1
Red Alligator - *Fell*	11.10-12	B. Fletcher	13/1
Specify - *Brought Down*	8.10-7	J. Cook	100/7
Two Springs - *Fell*	8.10-7	R. Edwards	13/2*
Battledore - *Brought Down*	9.10-5	T.S. Murphy	25/1
Rondetto - *Unseated Rider*	14.10-5	J. King	22/1
Fort Ord - *Fell*	10.10-5	A. Turnell	50/1
Permit - *Brought Down*	7.10-3	P. Buckley	35/1
French Excuse - *Fell*	8.10-2	K.B. White	100/8
The Otter - *Fell*	9.10-1	T.M. Jones	20/1
All Glory - *Fell*	9.10-0	A.L.T. Moore	50/1
The Beeches - *Fell*	10.10-0	S. Mellor	22/1
The Fossa - *Refused*	13.10-0	G.W. Robinson	50/1
Game Purston - *Unseated Rider*	12.11-5	Mr M.C. Loyd	100/1
No Justice - *Refused*	9.10-0	J. Guest	50/1
On The Move - *Fell*	8.10-1	G. Dartnall	100/1
Perry Hill - *Fell*	11.10-0	P. Kelleway	28/1
Persian Helen - *Refused*	7.10-0	D.T. Hughes	35/1
Queen's Guide - *Brought Down*	9.10-0	Mr G. Wade	40/1
Racoon - *Fell*	8.10-3	D. Mould	33/1
Villay - *Fell*	12.10-0	Mr D. Scott	100/1

Weight is in stones and pounds.

* Denotes favourite.

1971
SPECIFY

Despite falling on his first appearance of the new season, Gay Trip made it back to Aintree to defend his crown in 1971. His form throughout the campaign had been disappointing in general and now he would have to cope with a 9lb weight rise as he again headed the handicap. Although no horse had succeeded in consecutive Grand Nationals since Reynoldstown pulled off the double in 1936, Gay Trip, reunited with jockey Terry Biddlecombe this year, was made favourite for glory at 8/1.

Among thirty-seven challengers attempting to wrest away his crown was the impressive ten-year-old The Laird. Trained by Bob Turnell, The Laird had quality form to his name, having finished as runner-up in the 1968 Cheltenham Gold Cup, and had won his last three races – at Ascot, Kempton and Cheltenham. The Laird was accompanied to the Grand National by his stablemate, Charter Flight, who had gained valuable experience of the daunting fences when winning the Topham Trophy the year before and was no forlorn hope at 25/1.

The recent Cheltenham Festival had thrown forward a very interesting contender in the shape of Lord Jim. The horse was fresh from a mouth-watering success in the National Hunt Handicap Chase, which strongly outlined his Aintree credentials. Trained by Fulke Walwyn, Lord Jim had only been out of the first two places twice in his last fourteen runs.

Ireland had a particularly strong set of possibilities this year with Vulture and Miss Hunter, second and third in last year's race, ready for battle again together with a cluster of interesting newcomers. Among them were King Vulgan, well fancied after winning at Downpatrick the previous month, and Money Boat. The pair stood at 16/1 in the betting. Perhaps the most intriguing of the Irish runners was Black Secret. Trained by Tom Dreaper and ridden by his son Jim, an amateur, the horse had reeled off four consecutive victories earlier in the season. Although only a seven-year-old, Black Secret was a worthy challenger and lined up at a tempting 20/1.

Of those who did not get round in the previous year's race, Two Springs again was well fancied while The Otter, who had been going well when coming to grief, carried with him the extreme confidence of his stable. Specify was another who could be considered unlucky in the 1970 contest, as he was running a fine race just behind the leaders when brought down at the second Becher's. True enough, Specify did not have much recent form, but the horse had won a Mildmay of Flete Chase at the 1969 Cheltenham Festival and had clearly taken to the big Aintree fences last year. Despite these credentials, the John Sutcliffe-trained contender did not feature among the leading horses in the betting, being sent off as a 28/1 chance.

The excitement quickly mounted as the field was dispatched, and crossing the Melling Road and on towards the first fence, it was an outsider, Beau Bob, who led a group including Gay Buccaneer, Smooth Dealer, Flosuebarb and Limeburner. The first shock of the race came seconds later when favourite Gay Trip crashed at the opening flight, along with Craigbrock.

100/1 outsider Vichysoise ran better than expected to finish seventh.

As the field charged on, it emerged that Twigairy, Brian's Best and Country Wedding had been brought down as well.

At the third fence, The Laird joined Gay Trip as a well-backed casualty, and it was now Gay Buccaneer who had jumped to the front as the rest of the runners thundered down to, and swept over, Becher's Brook.

At the Canal Turn, Gay Buccaneer was carried extremely wide, surrendering the lead to Ireland's Miss Hunter with Smooth Dealer showing up nicely too. The chance of an outsider winning rose dramatically at fences ten and eleven when the well-fancied pair of The Otter and Lord Jim departed respectively. Their exits meant the first four in the betting market had now plummeted out of the race.

Miss Hunter still led at the Chair, but here her gallant run came to an abrupt end after she took off too early and failed to negotiate the beast of a fence. This left Astbury, Flosuebarb and Beau Bob to lead the field out for another circuit from The Inventor, Sandy Sprite and Limeburner.

On the run down to Becher's for the second time, it was Beau Bob out in front and jumping beautifully with Richard Dennard on board. But the most famous fence on the course was to prove ultimately calamitous for the jockey. Jumping the fence well enough, Beau Bob pecked slightly on landing, causing Dennard to slip slightly from the saddle and, as the horse careered on towards the twenty-third fence, the jockey was unseated in a swirl of Aintree frustration.

As they reached the Canal Turn again, ten horses were clear of the rest with the rank outsider Limeburner and the mare Sandy Sprite, who had been second in the season's Welsh Grand National, leading the way. Black Secret was going strongly, having survived a blunder at the previous fence, then came Astbury, The Inventor, Bowjeeno, Specify, Regimental, Two Springs and Vichysoise.

The seven-year old Sandy Sprite was travelling supremely for Ron Barry and, at the second last, looked the likely winner. At this fence Limeburner fell dramatically on the outside of the leaders, having run a splendid race for John Buckingham, but there were still others left to challenge Sandy Sprite – by the final fence, five horses still had a realistic chance.

The mare touched down in front, but she was being chased relentlessly by Black Secret and Bowjeeno, with Astbury on the outside and Specify starting to make a run on the inside.

At the elbow, the brave leader was engulfed once and for all, and in one of the best finishes to the Grand National ever, John Cook rallied Specify against the rails to beat Black Secret by a neck and emerge victorious from a dramatic five-horse battle. A couple of lengths back came Astbury from Bowjeeno and Sandy Sprite.

For jockey John Cook, it was victory in his third attempt at the race, and for trainer John Sutcliffe, a gigantic training achievement. Based in Epsom, Sutcliffe had a team of just eight jumpers, yet Aintree glory had been preceded recently by a first and second in the season's richest handicap hurdle, the Schweppes Gold Trophy.

As for Specify, he had been bought for £13,000 by Mr Fred Pontin after a chase win at Windsor the previous season. Unlucky not to recuperate the price tag in last season's race, Specify had done his owner proud this time around.

The unlucky horse of the race was undoubtedly Sandy Sprite. She had looked like becoming the first mare to win the National since Nickel Coin in 1951, but it was later discovered she had broken down in the later stages of the race and only sheer bravery had got her to the finish. It was left to her trainer John Edwards and jockey Ron Barry to dream of what might have been, while for Specify and his connections, they could now revel at their place in Grand National history.

HORSE/FATE	AGE/WEIGHT	JOCKEY	ODDS
1st **SPECIFY**	9.10-13	J. COOK	28/1
2nd **BLACK SECRET**	7.11-5	MR J. DREAPER	20/1
3rd **ASTBURY**	8.10-0	J. BOURKE	33/1
4th **BOWJEENO**	11.10-5	G. THORNER	66/1
5th Sandy Sprite	7.10-3	R. Barry	33/1
6th Two Springs	9.11-4	R. Edwards	13/1
7th Vichysoise	9.10-3	P. Blacker	100/1
8th King Vulgan	10.11-0	J. Crowley	16/1
9th Regimental	8.10-6	Mr J. Lawrence	66/1
10th Gay Buccaneer	10.10-0	P. Black	66/1
11th Final Move	11.10-0	T. Stack	66/1
12th Limeburner	10.10-0	J. Buckingham - *Remount*	100/1
13th Common Entrance	10.10-0	Mr M. Morris - *Remount*	100/1
Gay Trip - *Fell*	9.12-0	T. Biddlecombe	8/1*
The Laird - *Fell*	10.11-12	J. King	12/1
Charter Flight - *Pulled Up*	9.11-8	W. Rees	25/1
Brian's Best - *Brought Down*	11.10-11	R. Evans	33/1
Cnoc Dubh - *Fell*	8.10-11	T. Carberry	20/1
Lord Jim - *Fell*	10.10-9	S. Mellor	9/1
The Inventor - *Refused*	10.10-7	B. Fletcher	20/1
Money Boat - *Fell*	7.10-7	R. Coonan	16/1
Soldo - *Fell*	10.10-7	D. Mould	66/1
Battledore - *Refused*	10.10-6	J. Enright	45/1
Twigairy - *Brought Down*	8.10-6	E.P. Harty	25/1
Beau Bob - *Unseated Rider*	8.10-3	R. Dennard	40/1
Smooth Dealer - *Refused*	9.10-3	A.L.T. Moore	33/1
The Otter - *Fell*	10.10-1	T.M. Jones	12/1
Copperless - *Fell*	10.10-1	M. Gibson	100/1
Country Wedding - *Brought Down*	9.10-0	R. Champion	50/1
Flosuebarb - *Pulled Up*	11.10-1	J. Guest	33/1
Craigbrock - *Fell*	12.10-1	P. Ennis	80/1
Highworth - *Pulled Up*	12.10-5	Mr R.H. Woodhouse	100/1
Indamelia - *Fell*	8.10-5	Mr P. Hobbs	100/1
Kellsboro' Wood - *Fell*	11.10-0	A. Turnell	100/1
Miss Hunter - *Fell*	10.10-0	Mr J. Fowler	33/1
Pride Of Kentucky - *Brought Down*	9.10-0	A. Mawson	50/1
Vulture - *Fell*	9.10-0	S. Barker	16/1
Zara's Grove - *Fell*	8.10-0	G. Holmes	66/1

1972
WELL TO DO

Back in 1965, the owner of Aintree racecourse, Mrs Mirabel Topham, had announced her intention to sell the course to property developers. Although that had never materialised, ever since the future of the Grand National had been unresolved and apparently doomed. Although the 1972 race was to receive sponsorship for the first time since the 1963 running – through BP Limited, making it the richest ever edition of the race – the long-term presence of the National was hanging by a thread and, not for the first time, the Grand National of 1972 was labelled the last ever to be run.

Returning to Aintree for the third consecutive year was the previous season's victor, Specify. Similar to the build-up he endured prior to the 1971 contest, Specify's form had been disappointing this season and he had failed to win a single race. Clearly though, the horse saved his best performances for Aintree, and that fact was not lost on punters, who sent the ten-year-old off just outside the market leaders at 22/1 for repeat glory.

Black Secret was back again as one of ten hopefuls from Ireland. The horse was well fancied to go one better than last year's showing, although Tom Dreaper's eight-year-old had not won a race since losing his titanic battle with Specify the previous April.

Enhancing the whole picture of the 1972 Grand National was the dominating presence of L'Escargot. Trained in Ireland by Dan Moore, the high-class nine-year-old was a two-time winner of the Cheltenham Gold Cup. His past glories earned him the hefty burden of 12st top weight; still L'Escargot attracted serious attention in the betting market and started at 17/2 favourite in his first attempt at the race.

After his early departure in the previous year's race, the 1970 winner Gay Trip had returned to form this season. The horse had claimed another Mackeson Gold Cup and had once more run well in the Cheltenham Gold Cup. Even though he was spared the mantle of top weight this time, Gay Trip would still have to carry a considerable 11st 9lb if he was going to grab back his crown.

Having his first ride in the race was John Francome, a rider of limitless potential. Partnering him on his inaugural venture was the highly-rated Cardinal Error, a quality jumper who had racked up four wins in the run up to Aintree. He shared second place in the betting at 12/1 with Gay Trip.

A host of horses having their first attempts at the National were well fancied and held prominent positions in the market. These included Fortina's Palace, Fair Vulgan, Well To Do, Gyleburn and Cloudsmere. The ultra-consistent Fortina's Palace had filled second place five times during the season and was regarded as a safe jumper. Fair Vulgan was a horse that liked to dictate the pace of a race and had proved his ability over long distances when taking the season's Eider Chase. Cloudsmere had won three recent races, Well To Do had the assistance of reigning

Fortina's Palace was a leading contender in the ultra-competitive 1972 edition.

champion jockey, Graham Thorner, while Gyleburn had enjoyed a steady campaign, taking Well To Do as one of his victims. Of the group, the public appeared particularly enamoured with the Tim Forster-trained chestnut Well To Do, and twenty-three-year-old Thorner's mount was relentlessly backed down to 14/1, having been 33/1 on the Friday and 25/1 on the Saturday morning of the race.

A piercing Merseyside wind was accompanied by lashings of rain as the big field of forty-two runners lined up at the start. Once they had set off, Fair Vulgan was quick to take up a position at a head of affairs and the front-runner was the first to rise at the opening fence. All bets staked on Gyleburn were quickly losing ones as he sent Ron Barry sprawling at the first.

Favourite backers knew their fate two fences later when L'Escargot was knocked rudely out of the race while the much-fancied Cardinal Error was so badly baulked that Francome's first assault on Aintree was soon over.

With a bunch of leading players already down and out, Fair Vulgan continued the march down to Becher's Brook, closely patrolled by Miss Hunter, General Symons, Astbury and Specify. A trio of outsiders in Swan-Shot, Beau Parc and Lisnaree all fell here as the leader bounded on.

Still out in front at the Water Jump, Fair Vulgan suffered serious interference from a loose horse. Surviving the incident, the leader carried on, but by the eighteenth, he was beginning to tire, with challengers in abundance ready to pounce. Miss Hunter, Bright Willow, Black Secret, General Symons, Astbury, Rough Silk, Specify and Gay Trip were all right in contention on the second circuit, along with Well To Do, who had been taken along the inside route by Thorner.

Black Secret now took up the running, fuelling Irish hopes still recovering from L'Escargot's shock exit, and the field headed again for Becher's, with Specify well positioned at the fence for the third straight year. Four others were going very well just behind and these were Gay Trip, Well To Do, Astbury and General Symons.

The action was hotting up all the time, and at Valentine's the race developed in to a four-horse contest between Gay Trip, Well To Do, Black Secret and General Symons.

Surprisingly, it was 40/1 outsider General Symons who landed in front two fences from home, his big, white face nosing ahead of Gay Trip on his outside. Black Secret was under extreme pressure to stay in touch, but Well To Do was travelling best of all on the inside and, jumping the last, Graham Thorner sent him clear.

Terry Biddlecombe, however, had not given up on former winner Gay Trip and he tried to rally his mount for one last charge. Passing the elbow and running up the centre of the track, Gay Trip made his presence felt, but Well To Do, sticking to the inside rails and in receipt of an invaluable 22lb, stayed on stronger to win a fantastic race.

Behind the first two, the game General Symons and Black Secret crossed the line together, and a dead heat was announced for third. Specify had not been able to stay with the leading quartet over the final stages, but had once again proven his desire for the challenge of Aintree, coming home a respectable sixth.

Gyleburn, another well-fancied prospect that failed to finish.

Having been represented by Bowjeeno's fourth place in 1971, Tim Forster and Graham Thorner had won the National at their second attempt, but it could of all been so different.

Forster had been bequeathed Well To Do in the will of Mrs Heather Sumner; she had brought him when he was a three-year-old. Uncertain whether to risk the horse at Aintree, Forster only entered Well To Do at the last minute, and when the chestnut could only finish second on his last outing at Ludlow, the doubts remained as to whether he would make the line up at all.

Ultimately though he did, and emotionally for Forster, the horse prevailed in the very race that had been the dream of his previous owner before she had died. The one sadness was that Mrs Sumner never got to witness Well To Do transforming her dreams into a glorious reality.

HORSE/FATE	AGE/WEIGHT	JOCKEY	ODDS
1st WELL TO DO	9.10-1	G. THORNER	14/1
2nd GAY TRIP	10.11-9	T.W. BIDDLECOMBE	12/1
3rd = BLACK SECRET	8.11-2	S. BARKER	14/1
3rd = GENERAL SYMONS	9.10-0	P. KIELY	40/1
5th Astbury	9.10-0	J. Bourke	25/1
6th Specify	10.10-11	B. Brogan	22/1
7th Bright Willow	11.10-1	W. Smith	28/1
8th Money Boat	8.10-3	F. Berry	16/1
9th Rough Silk	9.10-6	D. Nicholson	25/1
L'Escargot - *Knocked Over*	9.12-0	T. Carberry	17/2*
Alaska Fort - *Brought Down*	7.10-13	H.R. Beasley	33/1
Rigton Prince - *Pulled Up*	11.10-9	J. Enright	25/1
Twigairy - *Pulled Up*	9.10-9	T.G. Davies	28/1
Fortina's Palace - *Fell*	9.10-7	J. King	16/1
The Pantheon - *Fell*	9.10-4	K.B. White	33/1
Pearl Of Montreal - *Pulled Up*	9.10-4	R. Coonan	55/1
Swan-Shot - *Fell*	9.10-3	P. McCarron	33/1
Gyleburn - *Fell*	9.10-4	R. Barry	20/1
The Inventor - *Refused*	11.10-2	W. Shoemark	33/1
Cardinal Error - *Refused*	8.10-4	J. Francome	12/1
Saggart's Choice - *Fell*	9.10-1	T. Stack	28/1
Deblin's Green - *Pulled Up*	9.10-0	D. Cartwright	33/1
Nephin Beg - *Pulled Up*	10.10-0	P. Morris	100/1
Cloudsmere - *Fell*	8.10-4	D. Mould	18/1
Kellsboro' Wood - *Fell*	12.10-0	A. Turnell	100/1
Permit - *Fell*	9.10-0	R.R. Evans	100/1
Lime Street - *Fell*	8.10-1	R. Pitman	25/1
Just A Gamble - *Fell*	10.10-1	P. Buckley	100/1
Lisnaree - *Fell*	9.10-0	Mr F. Turner	100/1
Nom De Guerre - *Fell*	10.10-0	J. Haine	33/1
Gay Buccaneer - *Fell*	11.10-0	T. Hyde	33/1
Miss Hunter - *Pulled Up*	11.10-0	A.L. Moore	50/1
Vichysoise - *Refused*	10.10-3	P. Blacker	100/1
The Otter - *Fell*	11.10-0	T.M. Jones	25/1
Bullucks Horn - *Refused*	9.10-0	Mr R. Smith	28/1
The Pooka - *Fell*	10.10-5	Mr C. Ross	50/1
Fair Vulgan - *Fell*	8.10-0	M.C. Gifford	14/1
Beau Parc - *Fell*	9.11-2	Mr A. Nicholson	50/1
Even Delight - *Pulled Up*	7.10-2	R. Dennard	40/1
Limeburner - *Pulled Up*	11.10-0	W. Rees	100/1
Vulture - *Refused*	10.10-2	P. Brogan	100/1
Country Wedding - *Fell*	10.10-4	R. Champion	50/1

1973
RED RUM

So often in the world of sport, the victorious are thrust in to the spotlight, justifiably receiving their moments of glory. The winners are showered with praise while the defeated are left to ponder what might have been, rarely given more than sympathetic recognition. In general, the Grand National follows this path. Every year a jubilant hero is led in to the winner's enclosure surrounded by a mass of cheering onlookers, while all around, beaten horses are returned to those associated with them, largely cast aside in the wake of another's triumph. However, the remarkable Grand National of 1973 proved that while winners will always be remembered, those conquered should never be forgotten.

In the lead up to the race, Mrs Mirabel Topham, whose family had run the Grand National at Aintree since 1899, announced once and for all that the 1973 race would be the last running staged under their name. Mrs Topham revealed that plans for the sale of the race-course would be put into action after the Grand National, again casting doubts over the future of the race.

As if to literally prove that the great race categorically belonged to the famous Aintree turf, a galaxy of equine stars graced the field in 1973 – a line-up as good as any that the National had ever witnessed.

As joint top weight, the Australian-bred chaser Crisp was an exciting leading contender. Having excelled himself in both Australia and America, the ten-year-old had arrived in England two years previously and was now under the watch of trainer Fred Winter. The season before, Crisp had won four of his seven starts, while this season he had been given four outings on the build up to Aintree. With most of his performances coming between two and two-and-a-half miles, the one worry over Crisp was his ability to see out the gruelling distance of the National.

Joining him at the top of the handicap was L'Escargot. The horse was apparently none the worse for being knocked over in the previous year's race and had recently finished fourth in the Cheltenham Gold Cup.

With only two of last year's principal performers running this time around, those being joint thirds Black Secret and General Symons, the prospect of a new winner looked rock-solid. There were certainly plenty of challengers with their eyes fixed on glory.

Local trainer Donald McCain had two of the prospects that were new to the race. Glenkiln had won over the big fences at the meeting in October, beating L'Escargot on that occasion and was an intriguing each way prospect at 33/1. But it was his stable-mate Red Rum who had captured most public attention. The eight-year-old had been laid out for this very race and earlier in the season had recorded five wins on the trot. Then, given a winter break by McCain, Red Rum did well enough in his three runs leading up to the National to make himself 9/1 joint favourite with Crisp. To further aid his quest, Red Rum was ridden by Brian Fletcher, Red Alligator's successful pilot in 1968.

Also holding prominent positions in the market were Ashville and Princess Camilla. Ashville was trained in Newmarket by Tom Jones and had caught the eye when staying on strongly for second place in the National Hunt Handicap Chase at the Cheltenham Festival, while Princess Camilla had long been a leading fancy for the National. Winner of three races during the season, the mare had proven her stamina in her latest success over four miles and a furlong at Warwick. Her owner, John Bigg, was confident of a big run.

Adding an extra splash of class to the field were two powerful contenders, Spanish Steps and Grey Sombrero. Spanish Steps was owned and trained by Mr Edward Courage and would be carrying a mighty 11st 13lb, while the talented David Gandolfo-trained Grey Sombrero was expected to relish the fast going at Aintree. The grey horse had already won a Whitbread Gold Cup and a Midlands Grand National, so his stamina was not expected to be a worry.

Not knowing if they would be the last ever competitors to do so, the thirty-eight strong field charged down the Aintree turf and across the Melling Road, having been unleashed at the start of the 1973 Grand National.

At the first fence, Crisp and jockey Richard Pitman survived an early mistake while 50/1 shot Richeleau suffered the first fall of his life. At the third fence, Ashville made an unwanted exit, leaving jockey Jeff King to rue the obstacle. The rider had only got past the big ditch once in four years.

At the head of affairs, Crisp was settling down in to a beautiful rhythm, but Becher's Brook was to prove the downfall of outsiders Culla Hill, Beggar's Way and Mr Vimy. Meanwhile, Crisp was widening his advantage at every fence with fast, accurate jumping and by the Canal Turn had put a fair distance between himself and the chasing Grey Sombrero.

Going further and further in front, Crisp held a lead of over twenty lengths as he soared the Chair in majestic fashion. Behind him though, and clear of the main pack himself at the time, the gallant Grey Sombrero was about to take a fatal fall. Jumping the fence boldly, the grey landed awkwardly and appeared to stumble clumsily for a number of strides before capsizing. Although rising gingerly to his feet, the brave horse had broken a shoulder and had to be put down. This tragic twist left Crisp even further in front at the Water, with Endless Folly, Red Rum, Rouge Autumn and Sunny Lad now heading a large pack of pursuers.

Although Crisp must have seemed like a speck on the horizon, it was Red Rum who took the initiative in going after the leader and broke clear of the rest after jumping the big ditch second time round. However, Crisp was still tearing away relentlessly and he flew Becher's again going as strong as ever and continued his exhibition of jumping over the Canal Turn and Valentine's Brook.

Red Rum had gone well clear of the others now, with Spanish Steps, Hurricane Rock, Rouge Autumn, Black Secret and Great Noise the closest to him, but he had plenty to do to get anywhere near Crisp, who was twenty lengths in front.

It was only on the run to the second last that Crisp started to waver. The long-time leader had not seen another horse in the race, but he was obviously getting tired now. Like a shark sensing blood, Red Rum was cutting the leader down all the time, but even though Crisp ploughed through the last, he still had a commanding lead approaching the elbow.

The distress signs were now blatantly apparent in Crisp, however, and suddenly, he was hardly running at all, veering agonisingly towards the bordered off Chair. Pitman was working furiously as he straightened up his mount and tried to coax him in to one last effort. Red Rum was finishing much the stronger though, with 23lb less to carry and Crisp could not hold him off. Getting up in the last few strides, Red Rum won an enthralling duel by three quarters of a length.

The pair had the race to themselves and though he stayed on well at the finish, L'Escargot was twenty-five lengths back in third with Spanish Steps fourth.

The crowd had erupted after seeing the local challenger win the day and it was a true testament to Red Rum's trainer McCain that the horse had been in the race at all.

Having been bought by McCain on behalf of Mr Noel le Mare, it was soon realised that a serious foot disease had been dogging Red Rum. McCain took the horse to the salty waters of Southport Beach for regular gallops and it was here the horse came to life, losing his wretched ailment. With the lameness shaken off, Red Rum had then been prepared for his assault on Grand National history.

Brian Fletcher had won the day again, having been deeply concerned crossing the Melling Road for the final time that Crisp would not be caught. For Richard Pitman, all that was left was to reflect, having ridden a horse that had given him a magnificent ride and had helped him break Golden Miller's longstanding course record, set in 1934.

The 1973 race brought together two tremendous heroes who fought out one of the finest battles ever seen at Aintree. They had both shown fantastic courage, Crisp giving a superb spectacle of jumping and leading for all but the last few strides, while Red Rum showed tenacious fighting spirit to claw Crisp back from an impossible looking deficit.

For Crisp, defeat was a cruel price to pay for such a performance. For Red Rum though, it was just the beginning of a legendary era.

Red Rum is led into the winner's enclosure in 1973, having outlasted Crisp.

HORSE/FATE	AGE/WEIGHT	JOCKEY	ODDS
1st RED RUM	8.10-5	B. FLETCHER	9/1*
2nd CRISP	10.12-0	R. PITMAN	9/1*
3rd L'ESCARGOT	10.12-0	T. CARBERRY	11/1
4th SPANISH STEPS	10.11-13	P. BLACKER	16/1
5th Rouge Autumn	9.10-0	K.B. White	40/1
6th Hurricane Rock	9.10-0	R. Champion	100/1
7th Proud Tarquin	10.10-11	Lord Oaksey	22/1
8th Prophecy	10.10-3	B.R. Davies	20/1
9th Endless Folly	11.10-0	J. Guest	100/1
10th Black Secret	9.11-2	S. Barker	22/1
11th Petruchio's Son	10.10-5	D. Mould	50/1
12th The Pooka	11.10-0	A.L. Moore	100/1
13th Great Noise	9.10-2	D. Cartwright	50/1
14th Green Plover	13.10-0	Mr M.F. Morris	100/1
15th Sunny Lad	9.10-3	W. Smith	25/1
16th Go-Pontinental	13.10-4	J. McNaught	100/1
17th Mill Door	11.10-5	P. Cullis	100/1
Grey Sombrero - Fell	9.10-9	W. Shoemark	25/1
Glenkiln - Fell	10.10-7	J.J. O'Neill	33/1
Beggar's Way - Fell	9.10-1	T. Kinane	33/1
Canharis - Brought Down	8.10-1	P. Buckley	16/1
General Symons - Pulled Up	10.10-0	P. Kiely	33/1
Highland Seal - Pulled Up	10.10-6	D. Nicholson	20/1
Mr Vimy - Pulled Up	10.10-2	J. Haine	100/1
Astbury - Pulled Up	10.10-2	J. Bourke	50/1
Swan-Shot - Refused	10.10-0	M. Blackshaw	100/1
Beau Parc - Pulled Up	10.10-1	A. Turnell	100/1
Ashville - Fell	8.10-4	J. King	14/1
Tarquin Bid - Fell	9.10-0	J. Bracken	100/1
Rough Silk - Pulled Up	10.10-0	T. Norman	66/1
Richeleau - Fell	9.10-0	N. Kernick	50/1
Princess Camilla - Refused	8.10-4	R. Barry	16/1
Rampsman - Pulled Up	9.10-0	D. Munro	100/1
Fortune Bay II - Fell	9.10-3	Mr G. Sloan	66/1
Charley Winking - Fell	8.10-0	Mr D. Scott	100/1
Proud Percy - Fell	10.10-0	R.R. Evans	100/1
Nereo - Pulled Up	7.10-3	Duke of Alburquerque	66/1
Culla Hill - Fell	9.10-7	Mr N. Brookes	100/1

1974
RED RUM

Aintree Racecourse had new owners by the time of the 1974 race. Mrs Topham had kept her word and sold the course in late 1973, to property developer Bill Davies and his company the Walton Group, for £3 million. Favourite for the first race under the new regime was the Arthur Stephenson-trained Scout. The eight-year-old stayer had won his last three races and had the assistance of Tommy Stack in the saddle. The fact that Scout had only a featherweight ten stone to carry increased his popularity, and a good deal of late money for the horse saw him climb to the top of the market at 7/1.

If he was going to win his second National in a row, Red Rum would have to do it carrying a massive twelve stone. His thrilling win over Crisp last year, coupled with four good wins in the current season, had seen the Southport-trained star shoot to the top of the Aintree handicap. Trained in much the same way as the previous campaign, Red Rum's outings during the season had included a brave second place when giving weight away in the Hennessy Gold Cup, clearly indicating a horse at the top of his form. But the statistics showed no horse carrying twelve stone had won the Grand National since Reynoldstown back in 1936. Chiefly for this reason, Red Rum was only third in the betting at 11/1.

Sandwiched between Scout and Red Rum in the market was the now eleven-year-old L'Escargot. The dual Cheltenham Gold Cup winner was looking to make it third time lucky in the National and he arrived at Aintree in cracking form, having run a fine second in the Cathcart Chase at the Festival. That race was over a distance too much on the short side for the Irish horse, but it had clearly sharpened him up as he now focused on National triumph. For L'Escargot's jockey, Tommy Carberry, this would be his tenth ride in the race.

Others who had taken part in 1973 had returned for another try on this occasion and they included Spanish Steps, Rouge Autumn and Princess Camilla. Spanish Steps was again carrying a big weight and was one of three horses to line up for Mr Edward Courage. Rouge Autumn had run a splendid race at a big price last year and was considered a lively each-way chance at 28/1, the same price as the mare Princess Camilla, who had disappointed her followers the previous year when refusing.

Royal Relief, who along with Quintus made up Mr Courage's trio, had twice won the Champion Chase at Cheltenham, and was the mount of Lord Oaksey. The furthest he had ever won though was two-and-a-half miles, so his stamina had to be questioned.

Among the other contenders, Straight Vulgan was an improving eight-year-old who had won well at Nottingham earlier in the season, while Deblin's Green had won the previous season's Welsh Grand National, been second in the same race this season, and, being a solid stayer, seemed ideal for the National. The field also contained a winner of Czechoslovakia's awesome steeplechase, the Velka Pardubicka, in 40/1 shot Stephen's Society.

The field of forty-two were dispatched shortly after Princess Camilla had entertained onlookers with a display of bucking and kicking, and the anticipation and hopes of so many rose as one with the horses at the first fence.

Red Rum with his trainer, Ginger McCain.

The dreams of Royal Relief were over almost before they had begun when Lord Oaksey's mount failed the first test. The 18/1 shot was followed out of the race by rank outsider Go-Pontinental at the third and by Sixer, who was brought down a fence later.

Up with the early running were Charles Dickens, Sunny Lad, Pearl Of Montreal, Rough Silk, Rouge Autumn and Glenkiln, and it was the outsider Charles Dickens and jockey Andy Turnell who led the big field over Becher's for the first time. There were no fallers at all at the famous Brook, but the Canal Turn was a trap that an unlucky quartet succumbed to. Those to go were Huperade and his owner-jockey John Carden, Argent, Karacola and the fancied Deblin's Green. By Valentine's Brook, the former hunter-chaser Rough House had also fallen.

As Charles Dickens continued the venture to the frightfully big Chair fence, both Red Rum and Scout were making progress and were easily in contention. A loose horse provided some anxious moments for Turnell, but surviving the situation, he and Charles Dickens cleared the obstacle and were headed for the second circuit in the lead together with a packed group of Vulgan Town, Rough Silk, Red Rum, Scout, L'Escargot, Pearl Of Montreal and Sunny Lad.

The field lost Straight Vulgan, who was well in touch with the leaders, when he fell at the eighteenth fence, and it was now Red Rum's turn to take command and he approached Becher's travelling ominously well.

Red Rum's jockey Brian Fletcher knew his mount idled when in front, but the hero of 1973 was going so well that he took the race to the others, of whom Spanish Steps was starting to pull into contention.

Red Rum and Fletcher suffered a scare five fences from home when the horse made an uncharacteristic and extremely rare mistake, his nose brushing the ground. But it failed to stop him in his tracks and, with Scout running desperately out of stamina, Red Rum bounded across the Melling Road for the final time from L'Escargot with Spanish Steps and Charles Dickens gamely trying to stay in the race.

Jumping the second-last four lengths ahead, Red Rum showed the same finishing power as he had to reel in Crisp last year, and he cleared the last flight to come home a majestic winner for the second consecutive year.

L'Escargot had improved a place on last season's effort and was seven lengths adrift in second, while outsider Charles Dickens had run totally above expectations to finish third. Spanish Steps once again ran a courageous race to claim fourth position. Rouge Autumn followed up his fifth place in 1973 with a seventh this time, while one place later came Nereo, ridden by the colourful Spanish amateur, the Duke of Alburquerque. The favourite, Scout, eventually came home in eleventh place having looked a real threat at one stage – much to the relief of bookmakers Ladbrokes; the firm stood to lose £1 million on the horse if he had won, courtesy of a major last-minute gamble.

While Red Rum's winning time was a full eighteen seconds slower than his win in 1973, he had achieved the near-impossible task of hauling twelve stone successfully over the thirty mighty fences. His win marked the first back-to-back victories since Reynoldstown in 1935 and 1936, and jockey Brian Fletcher became only the second rider of the century to score three Grand National wins, amulating the amateur Jack Anthony.

Such was the stature of Red Rum's win, he was immediately given a quote of 12/1 to complete a miraculous hat-trick in 1975, and the great horse was swiftly given the encouragement of owner Mr Noel le Mare, who fully intended sending his prize asset back to Aintree next April for a shot at immortality.

HORSE/FATE		AGE/WEIGHT	JOCKEY	ODDS
1st	RED RUM	9.12-0	B. FLETCHER	11/1
2nd	L'ESCARGOT	11.11-13	T. CARBERRY	17/2
3rd	CHARLES DICKENS	10.10-0	A. TURNELL	50/1
4th	SPANISH STEPS	11.11-9	W. SMITH	15/1
5th	Rough Silk	11.10-0	M.F. Morris	66/1
6th	Vulgan Town	8.10-8	J. Haine	35/1
7th	Rouge Autumn	10.10-0	K.B. White	28/1
8th	Nereo	8.10-6	Duke of Alburquerque	100/1
9th	San-Feliu	11.10-3	P. Buckley	22/1
10th	Norweigan Flag	8.10-0	J. Bourke	50/1
11th	Scout	8.10-0	T. Stack	7/1*
12th	Quintus	8.10-0	G. Thorner	33/1
13th	Dunno	10.10-1	Mr N. Mitchell	100/1
14th	Tubs VI	11.10-6	V. O'Brien	22/1
15th	Escari	8.10-2	P. Black	66/1
16th	Sunny Lad	10.10-4	D. Cartwright	20/1
17th	Princess Camilla	9.11-4	M. Blackshaw	28/1
Argent - *Brought Down*		10.11-10	R. Coonan	50/1
Royal Relief - *Fell*		10.11-6	Lord Oaksey	18/1
Huperade - *Fell*		10.10-12	Mr J. Carden	100/1
Straight Vulgan - *Fell*		8.10-8	R. Barry	15/1
Roman Holiday - *Pulled Up*		10.10-7	J. King	66/1
Rough House - *Fell*		8.10-6	Mr J. Burke	14/1
Bahia Dorada - *Pulled Up*		9.10-2	J. Guest	100/1
Glenkiln - *Fell*		11.10-2	R. Crank	50/1
Shaneman - *Unseated Rider*		9.10-2	B. Hannon	50/1
The Tunku - *Pulled Up*		8.10-1	R.R. Evans	100/1
Stephen's Society - *Pulled Up*		8.11-5	Mr C.D. Collins	40/1
Cloudsmere - *Carried Out*		10.10-4	P. Kelleway	100/1
Francophile - *Refused*		9.10-5	R. Pitman	16/1
Pearl Of Montreal - *Pulled Up*		11.10-0	T. Kinane	50/1
Deblin's Green - *Brought Down*		11.10-0	N. Wakley	25/1
Beau Bob - *Fell*		11.10-0	J. Glover	100/1
Sixer - *Brought Down*		10.10-0	M. Salaman	66/1
Culla Hill - *Fell*		10.10-8	Mr N. Brookes	100/1
Beggar's Way - *Refused*		10.10-2	V. Soane	66/1
Astbury - *Pulled Up*		11.10-0	Mr W. Jenks	66/1
Wolverhampton - *Pulled Up*		7.10-0	R. Quinn	25/1
Estoile - *Fell*		10.10-0	R. Hyett	66/1
Karacola - *Brought Down*		9.10-0	C. Astbury	100/1
Mill Door - *Fell*		12.10-2	J. McNaught	100/1
Go-Pontinental - *Fell*		14.10-0	J. Suthern	100/1

1975
L'ESCARGOT

Despite the prospect of local hero Red Rum making history as the only horse ever to win three Grand Nationals, the crowd that turned up on National day in 1975 was worryingly sparse. It seemed the hike in admission prices, in particular the £20 fee for the County Stand, had most to do with the low turnout. Obviously all was not going to plan for Bill Davies, now in his second year of ownership, who, despite securing a new sponsorship agreement with the *News of the World*, had been bombarded with harsh criticism of his Aintree leadership. In addition to those worries, his eight-year-old chaser, Wolverhampton, who had pulled up when representing the Aintree chief in the 1974 Grand National, collapsed and died while completing his preparation for this year's race, the day before the event.

Not only were the crowds on the small side, so was the field, with only thirty-one lining up this time around. Those supporters who did turn up, however, made sure that their hero Red Rum, who had headed the betting market for a full twelve months, went off one of the shortest-priced favourites of all time at 7/2. Red Rum had rounded off the previous season with an excellent win in the Scottish Grand National and the current campaign had yielded a further pair of victories for the ten-year-old. Giving a lot of weight away again to his major rivals, there were still a number of negative points to deter those who claimed a third victory was a mere formality. First, the horse had run well below expectations at Haydock Park on his National warm-up, and secondly, and probably more of a concern, was the state of the going. His National wins had both come on top of the ground, while conditions at Aintree on this occasion were described as 'dead'.

Dan Moore had L'Escargot back for one final try at Grand National glory. The high-class chestnut again had the assistance of jockey Tommy Carberry, and although he had been soundly beaten by Red Rum in the last two runnings of the race, he was receiving a handy 11lb from his big rival this time. No Irish horse had won the race since Mr What in 1958, and at twelve years of age, this was the last realistic chance of winning the great race that one of the best chasers of modern times would get.

L'Escargot was not the only former Cheltenham Gold Cup winner in the field. In a group priced at 20/1, which included Aintree veteran Spanish Steps, was another twelve-year-old, The Dikler. The horse was having his first taste of the National, and although he had not won a race throughout the season, The Dikler had notably captured a King George VI Chase and a Whitbread Gold Cup during a highly successful career.

Also new to the National line up were Land Lark, Money Market and Rag Trade. Land Lark was ridden by the 1972 hero Graham Thorner, while Money Market had won a Mildmay/Cazalet Chase, a worthy Grand National trial, and also been fourth in the Hennessy Gold Cup. Those two were priced at 14/1, while Rag Trade, an unlucky faller last time out, was 18/1 with John Francome on board.

Of those who had failed to complete the course in 1974, Rough House and Royal Relief were again well fancied. Rough House arrived at Aintree in fine form, having

L'Escargot on his way to victory in 1975. He would be the last Irish-trained winner for over two decades.

taken the Great Yorkshire Chase as one of his victories during the season, while Royal Relief had been runner up in all three of his latest contests.

The nerves of those participating were stretched to the limit before the race, as the eight-year-old Junior Partner spread a plate, holding up the start by fifteen minutes. With the 100/1 outsider Zimulator leading over the first fence, Junior Partner was soon out of the contest altogether when crashing out at the second. These early stages saw treble-seeking Red Rum well back in the field, staying out of any unnecessary trouble.

Zimulator's brief moment in the spotlight came to an abrupt halt at the fourth as he took a tumble, while a fence later, Rough House again found the spruce covered fences too much, as he took his second straight Grand National fall.

Glanford Brigg and Beau Bob were right among the leaders as the field zeroed in on Becher's for the first time. A pair of long shots, Barona and Spittin Image, failed to negotiate Aintree's famous Brook, while Andy Turnell's mount, April Seventh, suffered the misfortune of being brought down. Lord Oaksey had got six fences further than last year on Royal Relief, but he was again damning his luck as the horse fell at the seventh, the smallest fence of the lot, and it was also here that L'Escargot survived a mistake to remain in contention.

Glanford Brigg, under a big weight and with Martin Blackshaw on board, now took control of the race and they were still galloping strongly, leading the survivors to the Chair. Suddenly, faced with a group of loose horses charging randomly around the obstacle, it looked liked chaos was about to commence, yet with cool horsemanship, Blackshaw and the other leaders negotiated the fence as the rider-less animals thankfully continued on their way. Behind the leaders though, tragedy struck as Land Lark died instantly after colliding awkwardly in mid-flight with another runner, Glen Owen. It was a cruel end for a talented racehorse.

Glanford Brigg was still in charge on the second circuit until High Ken took over at the nineteenth. Snapping at the heels of the leaders though were the major players, including Red Rum, L'Escargot and The Dikler. Others going well at this point were Southern Quest, Beau Bob, Manicou Bay and Money Market.

High Ken's bid came to a crashing end at the fence before Becher's, and as they took the giant fence soon after, Southern Quest and Red Rum led, with outsider Beau Bob becoming, sadly, the second fatality of the race after breaking his neck in a heavy fall.

By Valentine's, Red Rum was in command and the real possibility of history being made was beginning to loom large. L'Escargot and Tommy Carberry were jumping beautifully just behind him though, with The Dikler, Spanish Steps and Southern Quest not yet out of the hunt. By the Melling Road, the race had developed into a battle between two great Aintree horses, Red Rum and L'Escargot, one bidding for a place in history, the other seeking to crown a glorious career.

Presented with his best chance of finally conquering his Aintree nemesis, it was to be the Irish raider who scooted clear after the pair had jumped the last fence together, and the blinkered horse passed the post fifteen lengths ahead of the beaten champion to seal a wonderful chasing career.

Spanish Steps ran his customary fine race in third, with newcomer Money Market edging out The Dikler for fourth place. Some way behind the winner trailed in Rag Trade, last of the ten to finish, but proving that he could handle the unique fences after his recent fall. Although his followers may have been initially disappointed with the absence of a Red Rum hat-trick, his trainer Donald McCain was quick to announce that the horse would be back for another go at glory twelve months on.

Even the most hardcore of Red Rum fans could not begrudge L'Escargot his crowning glory. Twice a Cheltenham Gold Cup winner, he had now added the most famous race in the world to his achievements at the fourth attempt and had given owner, Mr Raymond Guest, the Grand National triumph he had strived for two decades to possess. For jockey Carberry it was the culmination of an unbelievable catalogue of recent winning rides, which had also garnered him the Cheltenham Gold Cup and Irish Grand National.

As for the gallant L'Escargot, his spectacular career was now at a close, and as a fine gesture by Mr Guest, the newest Aintree king was given as a present to the wife of jubilant trainer, Dan Moore.

HORSE/FATE	AGE/WEIGHT	JOCKEY	ODDS
1st **L'ESCARGOT**	**12.11-3**	**T. CARBERRY**	**13/2**
2nd **RED RUM**	**10.12-0**	**B. FLETCHER**	**7/2***
3rd **SPANISH STEPS**	**12.10-3**	**W. SMITH**	**20/1**
4th **MONEY MARKET**	**8.10-13**	**J. KING**	**14/1**
5th The Dikler	12.11-13	R. Barry	20/1
6th Manicou Bay	9.10-7	R. Champion	40/1
7th Southern Quest	8.10-6	S. Shields	33/1
8th Glanford Brigg	9.11-4	M. Blackshaw	20/1
9th Hally Percy	11.10-0	M.C. Gifford	66/1
10th Rag Trade	9.10-4	J. Francome	18/1
Clear Cut - *Fell*	11.11-1	T. Stack	20/1
High Ken - *Fell*	9.11-1	B. Brogan	28/1
Royal Relief - *Fell*	11.11-1	Lord Oaksey	22/1
April Seventh - *Brought Down*	9.11-0	A. Turnell	28/1
Rough House - *Fell*	9.10-12	J. Burke	12/1
Barona - *Fell*	9.10-8	P. Kelleway	40/1
Even Dawn - *Pulled Up*	8.10-4	D. Mould	50/1
Ballyrichard Again - *Unseated Rider*	10.10-1	A. Webber	40/1
Land Lark - *Fell*	10.10-1	G. Thorner	14/1
Castleruddery - *Refused*	9.10-4	Mr T. Walsh	33/1
Shaneman - *Pulled Up*	10.10-8	Mr P. Greenall	100/1
Zimulator - *Fell*	8.10-0	Captain D. Swan	100/1
Feel Free - *Fell*	9.10-0	M. Salaman	66/1
Glen Owen - *Fell*	8.10-0	D. Atkins	22/1
Junior Partner - *Fell*	8.10-0	K.B. White	18/1
Rough Silk - *Refused*	12.10-8	Mr L. Urbano	28/1
Tudor View - *Brought Down*	9.10-0	G. McNally	100/1
Beau Bob - *Fell*	12.10-1	J. Glover	100/1
Kilmore Boy - *Fell*	9.10-2	P. Blacker	40/1
Ballyath - *Pulled Up*	9.10-0	J. Bouke	100/1
Spittin Image - *Fell*	9.10-0	M. Cummins	50/1

1976
RAG TRADE

If the attendance at the previous year's Grand National had proved bitterly disappointing, then the bumper crowd for the 1976 race was a most welcome and deserved turnaround. For merely a few months after stepping in to manage the course from Bill Davies until 1978, bookmakers Ladbrokes had successfully restored a large amount of enthusiasm for the event. One of the key areas the new management concentrated on was a focus on jump racing, limiting the amount of races run on the flat. As a result of their efforts, 42,000 people flocked through the gates – one of the biggest showings for years.

Despite again capturing the imagination of the public, and rightly so after three consecutive super efforts in the National, Red Rum returned to the race for a fourth time with only marginal form to enhance his claims. Topping the weights once more, Red Rum had not won a race for fourteen months and the recent rain at Aintree had done nothing to improve his chances. Still, his bid was backed with the usual confidence from his trainer, who sent the former winner into battle with a new pilot this time, Tommy Stack.

Favourite on the day was to be the winner of the previous season's Scottish Grand National, Barona. The horse had only got as far as the first Becher's in 1975, and his trainer Roddy Armytage had focused Barona's season at another crack at the National. The stamina-rich ten-year-old had run progressively each time during the season, and had really caught the eye when putting in a strong finish behind subsequent Cheltenham Gold Cup winner Royal Frolic at Haydock Park. Support for the horse was strongly maintained and he started as a warm 7/1 favourite.

Having jumped round safely, albeit in last place the season before, Rag Trade was back for another go under the direction of trainer Fred Rimell, already a three-time winner of the race. The horse had landed some decent prizes since the 1975 National, including the Midlands Grand National and, most recently, the Welsh Grand National. Like Barona, he had shown his liking for long distances, and the recent rain had certainly not deterred Rimell and his big-race jockey, John Burke.

Spanish Steps, Money Market and The Dikler – third, fourth and fifth in the previous year's race – were back for another tilt at Aintree, while three newcomers to the National received their fair share of attention too. These were Jolly's Clump, Tregarron and Prolan. Jolly's Clump had won three of his previous five races, including the last two, while Tregarron was in red-hot form, having taken his last three. The grey horse Prolan provided Ireland with a serious candidate to follow up L'Escargot's success of the year before, and the horse had certainly enhanced his credentials with a strong win at Cheltenham recently.

The huge crowd settled down to enjoy the spectacle of thirty-two runners charging towards the first of thirty fences. Spittin Image, a 66/1 outsider, led the hopefuls as they came towards their initial test, and here Ormonde Tudor and Huperade became the first of the National's inevitable victims.

Spittin Image and jockey Andy Turnell continued in the lead and together with another long-shot, Nereo and the fifty-seven-year-old Duke of Alburquerque, soared over Becher's

Brook in magnificent fashion. Stalking the leaders at the time, Tregarron became the first of the major fancies to depart, after being caught out by the landing side of the fence. The sprawling horse caused havoc when falling right into the path of Ceol-Na-Mara, who was badly impeded, while back in the field, Red Rum also had to be alert to sidestep the 12/1 chance. Away from this mini-drama, Glanford Brigg and Tudor View had also made their exits while Money Market, The Dikler and Rag Trade followed the two leaders to the seventh fence.

Nereo and his veteran rider were proudly disputing the lead when they reached the thirteenth, but the fence was destined to be an unlucky one for the partnership as Nereo made a slight error and sent his jockey crashing to a spine-chilling fall, leaving the rest of the field to gallop dangerously over the Spanish amateur. The fall was so severe that the Duke remained hospitalised for some time after the race with head injuries.

Nereo's exit left Spittin Image in the lead with Spanish Steps, Eyecatcher, Golden Rapper and Red Rum all in close attention, and taking the mighty Chair, Spittin Image and Spanish Steps touched down together as the large crowd looked on and cheered their particular fancy.

With the exception of Tregarron, all the market leaders still held every chance of glory as the second circuit got under way, and at the twentieth fence it was John Francome's mount, Golden Rapper, who surged up on the inside to take a strong grip on proceedings. The diminutive chaser was only a recent purchase for trainer Fred Winter, but heading down to Becher's and going extremely well, it looked like a shrewd investment.

But Becher's on the second time round so often changes the complexion of the National and, holding a definite advantage approaching the fence, Golden Rapper took a spiralling, head-first fall to crash spectacularly out of the race, leaving Francome marooned on the ground. Fortunately, the horse got up and ran away from his thumping tumble, but not before bringing down Prolan and Boom Docker in the process. All of a sudden, the events at Becher's had left a clear-cut group of ten marching on towards the Canal Turn. Spittin Image was still up front and was joined by Eyecatcher and Churchtown Boy. Much to the delight of the crowd, Red Rum was in the running and holding every chance, along with The Dikler, Rag Trade, Ceol-Na-Mara, Sandwilan, Spanish Steps and Barona.

The noise from the crowd began to increase with every jump, and none more so than when Red Rum went up to dispute the lead five fences from home. But this exciting running of the National was clearly going to have a hectic finish as no less than nine horses were still in touching distance of the lead as they crossed the Melling Road for the final time.

By the second last, four horses had made a mouth-watering line. Eyecatcher, Ceol-Na-Mara, Red Rum and Rag Trade were all poised to challenge for supremacy, with The Dikler trying desperately to stay with them just behind. But with the lattermost's efforts in vain, Ceol-Na-Mara was also left toiling as the three principals surged clear running to the last.

Now it was the mare Eyecatcher on the inside who began to tire and with the noise from the crowd ready to erupt like a simmering volcano, Red Rum landed in front over the last with Rag Trade on his outside. To the despair of Red Rum's supporters, it was Rag Trade who stole an advantage as they raced on towards the elbow and John Burke's mount was finishing with admirable power. Fighting to the death, Stack and Red Rum pushed for one

Although in front at the last, Red Rum was denied a third victory by Rag Trade (6). The mare, Eyecatcher, came third.

last effort, but it was to be Rag Trade's Grand National, and the ten-year-old outstayed the two-time hero to win by a couple of lengths. Brian Fletcher enjoyed another great National ride, steering home Eyecatcher for third, just in front of the dour Barona. Next came Ceol-Na-Mara, who had run a fine first National, having almost been knocked out of the race at Becher's first time, and The Dikler belied his advancing years to take sixth. Of the others, Jolly's Clump had disappointed but returned home very lame while Money Market collapsed after completing the course, but thankfully was revived with oxygen.

Fred Rimell had proved himself yet again as a master trainer of Grand National horses, this being his record fourth win after ESB, Nicolaus Silver and Gay Trip. He also became the first trainer to win both the Cheltenham Gold Cup and Grand National in the same season since the legendary Vincent O'Brien in 1953. Rimell had taken the honours at Cheltenham courtesy of Royal Frolic. Irish jockey John Burke had given Rag Trade a magnificent ride, making up for his two previous ventures in the race, both falls from Rough House. He had become the first jockey to pull off the Gold Cup/National double in the same year on different horses, while winning owner Mr Pierre 'Teasy Weasy' Raymond was tasting Aintree glory for the second time, having been triumphant with Ayala in 1963.

While the day belonged undeniably to the victorious Rag Trade, Red Rum had run his heart out again in defeat. With such a big weight, it took a supreme effort to even get as close as he did to the winner. While his hopes of pulling off an invincible treble seemed to be vanishing, trainer Donald McCain was again defiant in his view that the great warrior would be back again at Aintree as a twelve-year-old.

HORSE/FATE	AGE/WEIGHT	JOCKEY	ODDS
1st **RAG TRADE**	**10.10-12**	**J. BURKE**	**14/1**
2nd **RED RUM**	**11.11-10**	**T. STACK**	**10/1**
3rd **EYECATCHER**	**10.10-7**	**B. FLETCHER**	**28/1**
4th **BARONA**	**10.10-6**	**P. KELLEWAY**	**7/1***
5th Ceol-Na-Mara	7.10-6	J. Glover	22/1
6th The Dikler	13.11-7	R. Barry	25/1
7th Sandwilan	8.10-0	R. Hyett	100/1
8th Spittin Image	10.10-0	A. Turnell	66/1
9th Spanish Steps	13.10-2	J. King	22/1
10th Black Tudor	8.10-0	G. Thorner	50/1
11th Churchtown Boy	9.10-6	M. Salaman	33/1
12th Highway View	11.10-10	P. Black	33/1
13th Jolly's Clump	10.10-3	I. Watkinson	12/1
14th Money Market	9.11-0	R. Champion	12/1
15th Colondine	9.10-0	B. Forsey	60/1
16th Indian Diva	9.10-3	Mr N. Henderson	100/1
Glanford Brigg - *Fell*	10.11-3	M. Blackshaw	28/1
High Ken - *Fell*	10.10-12	M. Dickinson	33/1
Roman Bar - *Fell*	7.10-10	G. Newman	33/1
Golden Rapper - *Fell*	10.10-8	J. Francome	28/1
Perpol - *Pulled Up*	10.10-6	K.B. White	66/1
Prolan - *Brought Down*	7.10-3	M.F. Morris	13/1
Merry Maker - *Fell*	11.10-2	Mr A. Mildmay-White	50/1
Tregarron - *Fell*	9.10-1	C. Tinkler	12/1
Nereo - *Fell*	10.10-1	Duke of Alburquerque	100/1
Huperade - *Fell*	12.10-4	Mr J. Carden	100/1
Meridian II - *Fell*	9.10-0	J.J. O'Neill	33/1
Tudor View - *Fell*	10.10-0	C. Read	100/1
Ballybright - *Fell*	9.10-0	Mr S. Morshead	80/1
Thomond - *Brought Down*	11.10-3	Mr A.J. Wilson	100/1
Boom Docker - *Brought Down*	9.10-0	J. Williams	50/1
Ormonde Tudor - *Fell*	7.10-0	K. Bamfield	100/1

1977
RED RUM

The 1977 Grand National meeting saw the transition from a mixed meeting to one purely comprised of jumping. With each race being generously sponsored; the main event itself would award the victor with a prize of £41,000. These innovations were rewarded with a splendid field of forty-two runners for the big day on 2 April.

Amongst the starters was the recent Cheltenham Gold Cup winner Davy Lad, and the Dessie Hughes-ridden seven-year-old was well fancied to give Ireland its second National winner in three years and become the first horse since Golden Miller back in the 1930s to do the Gold Cup/National double. However, there was a lingering feeling that Davy Lad, well weighted on 10st 13lb, was a fortunate winner at Cheltenham, where his three main rivals failed to complete and a fourth, Summerville, broke down when travelling like the winner.

Perhaps for this reason, the money on the day was for the Fred Rimell-trained Andy Pandy, who would be ridden by John Burke. Andy Pandy had been in terrific form during the season, having won three of his last five races and was described by his trainer as being an athletic jumper with a lot of brain. The plunge on the eight-year-old saw him backed down to 15/2 favourite. Rimell, attempting to train his fifth winner of the race, was represented by three others, including The Pilgarlic, a half-brother to L'Escargot.

Gay Vulgan, trained by Fulke Walwyn, had won his last five races, including over four miles at Cheltenham in January, and was thought to have a major chance, while Winter Rain had run extremely well over the big fences in the Topham Trophy two years previously but had missed the last campaign through injury. However, the Michael Dickinson-ridden contender had progressed well through the season and was considered to have a lively chance.

The classy eight-year-old Zeta's Son had been ultra-consistent through the season and had picked up a Hennessy Gold Cup. However, his jockey Ron Barry was forced to miss the race through injury and the horse ideally wanted heavy ground to maximise his National chance. However, these conditions were unfortunately absent from Aintree on the day, and Mouse Morris was booked to take the unlucky Barry's place.

Among the other competitors, Sage Merlin and War Bonnet had both been in solid recent form, while Charlotte Brew, much to the concern of Red Rum's trainer Ginger McCain, was the first female rider to line up, partnering her own horse Barony Fort. Twenty-one-year-old Brew had backed herself at 50/1 to get round and was determined to complete, saying she would remount three times if need be.

Red Rum himself was twelve now and again shouldered top weight. He had not won for over six months and his recent form had been disappointing. However, he was, quite rightly, a firm fan-favourite, and those encouraged by McCain's recent verdict that the horse's last run at Haydock Park had delighted him and knowing that he saved his best for Aintree, joined in the backing of the old horse, sending him off 9/1 second favourite. Surely though, there were others at this stage with stronger designs on glory.

One of those was Churchtown Boy, running in his second National having been eleventh the previous year and who had bolted up over the big fences in the Topham Trophy on the Thursday. As a result, his odds for the National came crashing down from 100/1 to 20/1, as he attempted to become the first horse ever to do the double.

The sun shone brightly as the race began, in stark contrast to the days leading up to the event, which had been gloomy and wet. It was the Scottish-trained Sebastian V who was the leader at the first, and although he made it over safely, the obstacle marked the end for seven other warriors, including the fancied pair Pengrail and War Bonnet, and the easy-to-identify grey challenger, Willy What. Back in the pack, Gay Vulgan made a mistake that shook him severely and ruined his chances. Apparently, the big fences, according to jockey Bill Smith, had frightened him.

The big ditch shattered Davy Lad's National aspirations, and by the time the runners had cleared the fourth fence, the race had claimed thirteen of the forty-two starters. The awesome sight of Becher's Brook now lay in wait for the field, and it was Sebastian V that was blazing a trail down towards the fence, but the obstacle swept him off his feet on the landing side, while in the middle of the pack Winter Rain nose-dived and tragically broke his neck in a sickening fall.

All this had left outsider Boom Docker in front, and by the Canal Turn he had established a clear lead, one that he extended with every stride. With Prince Rock having cannoned his jockey from the saddle out in the country, Boom Docker was well clear of the pack as he approached the Chair, and while he sailed over with ease, Sage Merlin, who had himself been leading the remainder, crumpled on landing after hitting the top of the fence, much to the annoyance of jockey Ian Watkinson who later claimed that the horse was running away with him at the time. This left Andy Pandy to head the pursuit of the runaway leader, closely followed by What A Buck, Brown Admiral, Sir Garnet and Forest King. At this stage, Red Rum and Chrurchtown Boy were going very nicely just behind as the second circuit got under way.

However, like no other race, the National throws up the unexpected, and Boom Docker, with a monstrous advantage, dug his feet in and ground to a halt at the seventeenth, as if to say he had done enough. Boom Docker's untimely exit was the signal for Andy Pandy to ignite his National challenge. Now it was the favourite's turn to dictate proceedings and the anticipation grew as Andy Pandy drew clear himself, seemingly only having to stand up to give Rimell and Burke consecutive wins in the race. Jumping like a stag, he was a full ten lengths clear going to Becher's second time but, although he jumped the fence well, he could not stay upright on landing and his chance evaporated in front of the disbelieving spectators.

Now though, an even more fascinating story was unfolding as Red Rum, the horse who was considered past his best, was left in front with the field strung out. As What A Buck, Hidden Value and Forest King faded, it was Churchtown Boy who posed the chief threat to Tommy Stack and 'Rummy' as they jumped Valentine's and the fences beyond; by the second last, the two had come well clear. Churchtown Boy, with Martin Blackshaw on board, was seemingly going much the stronger but he clouted the second last and

Red Rum began to draw clear, the roars of the crowd seemingly magnetising the dual winner to the finish. He duly jumped the final fence and scorched up the run in to the most fantastic and deafening crescendo of applause to take his place in history as a glorious, unique three-time winner.

A now tired Churchtown Boy had given everything and came home second, with Eyecatcher again taking third place and The Pilgarlic staying on for fourth. Back out on the course, Charlotte Brew's dreams ended when Barony Fort refused.

Despite the tremendous reception he received from the huge upsurge in the race day crowd, not everyone was happy with Red Rum's triumph. A spokesman for bookmakers William Hill said that for them it was financially the worst result in the history of the race.

Sadly, the Grand National's darker side had surfaced with Zeta's Son becoming a second fatality after breaking a leg at Valentine's on the second circuit. However, the 1977 edition will always be remembered as the race which turned Red Rum into the all-time, undisputed legend of Aintree, and at this stage, McCain said it would be all systems go for an attempt at an unthinkable fourth win twelve months later.

A third victory elevated Red Rum to legendary status. A statue of the horse was erected near the winner's enclosure. After he died many years later, Red Rum was buried next to the winning post.

HORSE/FATE	AGE/WEIGHT	JOCKEY	ODDS
1st **RED RUM**	**12.11-8**	**T. STACK**	**9/1**
2nd **CHURCHTOWN BOY**	**10.10-0**	**M. BLACKSHAW**	**20/1**
3rd **EYECATCHER**	**11.10-1**	**C. READ**	**18/1**
4th **THE PILGARLIC**	**9.10-4**	**R.R. EVANS**	**40/1**
5th Forest King	8.10-12	R. Crank	33/1
6th What A Buck	10.11-4	J. King	20/1
7th Happy Ranger	10.10-5	P. Blacker	66/1
8th Carroll Street	10.10-0	R. Linley	50/1
9th Collingwood	11.10-1	C. Hawkins	50/1
10th Hidden Value	9.10-4	J. Bourke - *Remount*	40/1
11th Saucy Belle	11.10-0	R.F. Davies - *Remount*	200/1
Zeta's Son - *Fell*	8.11-4	M.F. Morris	18/1
Davy Lad - *Fell*	7.10-13	D.T. Hughes	10/1
Roman Bar - *Fell*	8.10-10	P. Kiely	25/1
Gay Vulgan - *Pulled Up*	9.10-8	W. Smith	9/1
Pengrail - *Fell*	9.10-8	R. Atkins	15/1
Andy Pandy - *Fell*	8.10-7	J. Burke	15/2*
Prince Rock - *Fell*	9.10-6	G. Thorner	18/1
War Bonnet - *Fell*	9.10-6	T. Carberry	16/1
Winter Rain - *Fell*	9.10-6	M. Dickinson	16/1
High Ken - *Brought Down*	11.11-3	Mr J. Edwards	50/1
Sir Garnet - *Unseated Rider*	8.10-3	J.J. O'Neill	20/1
Brown Admiral - *Fell*	8.10-1	S. Morshead	28/1
Duffle Coat - *Fell*	9.10-4	B.R. Davies	100/1
Lord Of The Hills - *Pulled Up*	10.10-1	D. Goulding	100/1
Nereo - *Fell*	11.10-0	R. Kington	100/1
Sage Merlin - *Fell*	9.10-5	I. Watkinson	20/1
Boom Docker - *Refused*	10.10-0	J. Williams	66/1
Castleruddery - *Fell*	11.10-0	L. O'Donnell	40/1
Harban - *Fell*	8.10-0	F. Berry	66/1
Sebastian V - *Fell*	9.10-1	R. Lamb	22/1
Royal Thrust - *Fell*	8.10-0	C. Tinkler	100/1
Burrator - *Fell*	8.10-0	Mr J. Docker	50/1
Sandwilan - *Refused*	9.10-0	R. Hyett	50/1
Foresail - *Refused*	10.10-0	G. Holmes	100/1
Inycarra - *Fell*	10.10-0	S. Jobar	100/1
Spittin Image - *Fell*	11.10-5	R. Champion	50/1
Willy What - *Fell*	8.10-0	J. Glover	50/1
Fort Vulgan - *Brought Down*	9.10-0	N. Tinkler	50/1
Barony Fort - *Refused*	12.10-1	Miss Charlotte Brew	200/1
Huperade - *Fell*	13.10-7	Mr J. Carden	200/1
The Songwriter - *Pulled Up*	8.10-0	B. Smart	200/1

1978
LUCIUS

The biggest of Grand National bombshells was dropped the day before the 1978 race when trainer Donald McCain revealed that the king of Aintree, Red Rum, would be missing from the field after picking up an injury in his final workout gallop. Now at thirteen years of age, it would undoubtedly be asking far too stern a question of the horse to return in 1979, so the wise decision was taken to retire the decorated local-legend from jump racing. The news robbed the race of its largest attraction, although Red Rum was invited to lead the parade before the National, giving him the opportunity to lap up the cheers of his adoring public one final time before settling in to a well-earned post-racing life. Even McCain was forced to admit Aintree would not be the same without the perennial challenger.

Red Rum's late withdrawal, together with that of last year's fifth Forest King, had left the 1978 event with an overall cast of newcomers to begin the 'post-Rummy' era. True, a pair of last season's placed horses, Churchtown Boy and The Pilgarlic returned once more, together with 1976 winner Rag Trade, but the thirty-seven-runner line-up generally had a fresh feel about it.

With so few of the runners having any previous National experience, it was an old hand who was turned to in the betting market, as punters latched on to Red Rum's nemesis of two years before, Rag Trade. The horse had been denied the chance to defend his crown in 1977 through injury and arrived for the race having also changed trainers since his most glorious achievement. Now under the guidance of George Fairbarn and ridden by Irishman Jonjo O'Neill, Rag Trade arrived at Aintree full of optimism having won his most recent race, and was readily made the 8/1 favourite.

In what appeared a wide-open Grand National, there was no shortage of contenders to capture the imagination. Most fancied of the first-timers happened to be the Irish challenger Tied Cottage. Placed three times during a consistent season, Tied Cottage was set to be guided round Aintree by L'Escargot's triumphant jockey, Tommy Carberry. Another in fine form prior to the Grand National was Master H. Trained in Worcestershire by Michael Oliver; the nine-year-old had won three of his last nine races and been runner-up in two of them. Ultra-confident that his mount would adapt to the unique perils of the course, jockey Reg Crank's hopes were highlighted by the fact that Master H had only once failed to complete a start in thirty-three runs and had sauntered round under a big weight at Worcester the previous week.

Grouped at 14/1 with last year's runner-up Churchtown Boy and Irish raider So, was the northern hope Lucius. Trained by Gordon Richards, Lucius was a recognised stayer who had chalked up a trio of victories on the way to the National. But his regular jockey would not partner him on this occasion: David Goulding had aggravated a back injury, ruling him out of contention, so the task of steering Lucius round fell to Bob Davies. Davies would only be getting his first feel for the horse in the pre-race paddock.

Others to command attention in the betting market were Shifting Gold, April Seventh and Sebastian V. A winner three times during the season, Shifting Gold had tarnished his reputation by falling last time out in the Grand National trial at Haydock Park. Now twelve, April Seventh was a previous winner of the Whitbread Gold Cup and the Hennessy Gold Cup, while the front-running Sebastian V had gone on to win the Scottish Grand National after falling at the first Becher's at Aintree the previous season.

After a youthful display of kicking and rearing from Red Rum in the parade, the field assembled at the start for the big event. As the race got underway, Tied Cottage immediately showed up boldly in front as he charged towards the first fence, followed by the thunderous procession of hooves pounding on the famous Aintree turf.

The dash to the first fence caused the expected untidy grief as Otter Way, along with outsiders Cornish Princess and Teddy Bear II, bit the dust at the most unenvied of exiting points. Tommy Stack, who had experienced all the joy possible in the race twelve months before, was soon picking himself off the ground after Hidden Value's fall at the second, as Tied Cottage continued to race away at the head of affairs, leading the field down to Becher's Brook.

With reckless abandon, Tied Cottage jumped the monstrous fence alarmingly to the left, and failing to survive the perilous drop on the landing side, was promptly down on the floor and out of the race. Henry Hall and Gleaming Rain also found the challenge of Becher's too much, as Double Bridal and Lucius were left to dictate the race out in front.

Two fences after Tied Cottage's bizarre exit, Master H became the next leading fancy to depart when darting swiftly to the right having just jumped the Canal Turn. With his saddle slipping, Reg Crank found himself being unseated in the most frustrating fashion. The bleak fate of more of the leading contenders was not far off. Having made a mistake at Valentine's, Shifting Gold fell at the very next fence along with the Irish challenger So, and with Rag Trade toiling, the situation appeared rosy for the bookmakers.

Going back on to the racecourse, Lucius was out in the lead from Drumroan, Sebastian V, Double Bridal, Lean Forward, Harban, Mickley Seabright and Roman Bar. Also going well was Churchtown Boy, but his race came to an end when falling at The Chair, leaving jockey Martin Blackshaw to hurl his whip to the ground in annoyance as yet another leading player fell by the wayside.

Going over the Water and journeying on towards circuit number two, Sebastian V and Lucius were both clearly enjoying themselves. One who was not though was Rag Trade, and as the remainder of the field were running down to Becher's again, the brave former winner was being pulled up by O'Neill, having suffered another untimely knock in an injury-plagued career.

Sebastian V led the survivors as they approached Becher's, with Lucius keeping him company. Drumroan and Roman Bar were in contention, while making eye-catching progress was Fred Winter's recruit Lord Browndodd, together with The Pilgarlic. Harban was another horse going well, but his dreams were soon over as he unseated his jockey jumping over the twenty-second flight, while Graham Thorner performed a miracle in recovering Tamalin from a hopeless-looking mistake – although the error cost him a great deal of ground. The leaders remained intact as they jumped Valentine's and beyond, Sebastian V still giving a bold display of fencing, and as the race progressed round the final turn, a plethora of runners still had their dreams very much alive.

Sebastian V was showing no signs of stopping as they arrived at two out, with Lucius and Lord Browndodd snapping at his heels and Coolishall now travelling smoothly on the extreme outside. The Pilgarlic, Drumroan, Mickley Seabright and The Songwriter had most to do out of those still in contention.

With Lord Browndodd starting to fade, it was the Martin O'Hallaran's mount Coolishall who appeared ready to unleash a winning run at the last fence, but first he would have to get by long-time leaders Sebastian V and Lucius.

As they flew over the last, five horses settled down to fight out a pulsating finish. Lucius edged in front of Sebastian V and his jockey Riddley Lamb, and with Coolishall's bid failing to materialise and The Pilgarlic unable to reach the front two down the inside, it was Drumroan who came from the back of the group to make a late charge at the leaders. His challenge, however, was to be in vain, as Lucius was to prove the strongest of all in a thrilling climax, and he held on to pip the game Sebastian V by half a length. Drumroan had finished in blitzing fashion and so nearly had given trainer Peggy St John Nolan the distinct honour of being the first lady to train the Grand National winner. The horse, though, had to settle for third place in front of Coolishall and The Pilgarlic.

A fantastic and deeply competitive renewal of the race had been won by Lucius, who Gordon Richards had purchased as an unbroken three-year old on behalf of the horse's owner, Mrs Fiona Whitaker. Changes affecting Aintree's future appeared forthcoming as the course was put up for sale on the Monday after the race at an asking price of £2.5million. The public interest in the National, however, was as strong as ever, with a huge crowd of 57,000 present at Aintree on the Saturday. The biggest crowd since the early 1950s made Grand National day a blend of colour and excitement, and many of the vast crowd were on hand to welcome Lucius in to the winner's enclosure as the newest hero of the great race.

Lucius is mobbed after holding off Sebastian V and Drumroan in a thrilling finale.

HORSE/FATE	AGE/WEIGHT	JOCKEY	ODDS
1st **LUCIUS**	**9.10-9**	**B.R. DAVIES**	**14/1**
2nd **SEBASTIAN V**	**10.10-1**	**R. LAMB**	**25/1**
3rd **DRUMROAN**	**10.10-0**	**G. NEWMAN**	**50/1**
4th **COOLISHALL**	**9.10-0**	**M. O'HALLORAN**	**16/1**
5th The Pilgarlic	10.10-1	R.R. Evans	33/1
6th Mickley Seabright	10.10-3	Mr P. Brookshaw	33/1
7th Lord Browndodd	10.10-7	J. Francome	16/1
8th The Songwriter	9.10-0	B. Smart	50/1
9th Roman Bar	9.10-8	P. Kiely	33/1
10th Brown Admiral	9.10-0	J. Burke	33/1
11th Golden Whin	8.10-4	S. Holland	50/1
12th Tamalin	11.11-2	G. Thorner	25/1
13th Lean Forward	12.10-0	H.J. Evans	33/1
14th Nereo	12.10-0	M. Floyd	66/1
15th Never Rock	9.10-0	K. Mooney	50/1
Shifting Gold - *Fell*	9.11-6	R. Champion	16/1
Tied Cottage - *Fell*	10.11-4	T. Carberry	9/1
Rag Trade - *Pulled Up*	12.11-3	J.J. O'Neill	8/1*
Master H - *Unseated Rider*	9.11-2	R. Crank	10/1
April Seventh - *Refused*	12.10-11	A. Turnell	20/1
Otter Way - *Fell*	10.10-10	J. King	16/1
War Bonnet - *Fell*	10.10-8	D.T. Hughes	50/1
So - *Fell*	9.10-4	Mr N. Madden	14/1
Hidden Value - *Fell*	10.10-0	T. Stack	25/1
Master Upham - *Fell*	10.10-0	P. Barton	25/1
Irish Tony - *Fell*	10.10-0	D. Atkins	33/1
Double Negative - *Fell*	8.10-0	C. Tinkler	33/1
Churchtown Boy - *Fell*	11.10-0	M. Blackshaw	14/1
Cornish Princess - *Fell*	10.10-1	R. Hoare	66/1
Harban - *Unseated Rider*	9.10-0	J.P .Byrne	66/1
Henry Hall - *Fell*	9.10-0	F. Berry	66/1
Burrator - *Fell*	9.10-0	J. Suthern	66/1
Double Bridal - *Fell*	7.10-1	W. Smith	50/1
Teddy Bear II - *Fell*	11.10-4	P. Blacker	50/1
Silkstone - *Fell*	10.10-0	G. Graham	66/1
Gleaming Rain - *Fell*	10.10-0	S. Treacy	25/1
Sadale VI - *Fell*	11.10-1	C. Candy	66/1

1979
RUBSTIC

Thankfully, Ladbrokes had by this time agreed with Bill Davies to extend their management of the course until 1982, allowing Grand National lovers everywhere to relax, if only for the time being, with the event in safe hands. With only 10st 13lb to carry in the 1979 Colt Car Company-sponsored Grand National, the recent Cheltenham Gold Cup winner Alverton was presented with a glorious chance of becoming the first horse to capture the Gold Cup and Grand National in the same season since Golden Miller in 1934.

The previous year's winner Lucius had been ruled out just days before the race with a cough, and this had left Alverton to receive most of the attention in the betting. Nagging doubts lingered over Alverton's ability to jump round Aintree though, and even his jockey Jonjo O'Neill admitted the horse would have to gain more height at his fences if he was going to conquer the ultimate challenge. Even so, a consistent flow of money saw the nine-year-old priced as the 13/2 favourite.

Having already masterminded the victories of four previous National heroes, Fred Rimell had a strong-looking quartet to represent him this time. Most fancied of his runners was The Pilgarlic, fifth in last season's race. The Pilgarlic had been sent hunting during the season, and after winning his last race, the Aintree veteran was sent off a 16/1 chance. Completing Rimell's team were the 1976 Cheltenham Gold Cup winner Royal Frolic, who carried top weight, nine-year-old Godfrey Secundus and outsider Double Negative.

Another trainer who had previously experienced winning the great race was Tim Forster. The man responsible for Well To Do's success in 1972 had a powerful duo to go to war with this time in Mr Snowman and Ben Nevis. Mr Snowman, an impressive jumper, had not been out of the places in his last six runs and had been lightly raced during the season. The consistent horse was the mount of Graham Thorner, and the partnership held second place in the betting at 10/1. Ben Nevis was also well fancied after showing steady improvement for his trainer since his arrival from the United States of America. The eleven-year-old was a former winner of the highly regarded Maryland Hunt Cup and would be ridden in the National by amateur Mr Charlie Fenwick.

Coolishall's bold effort in last year's National saw him receive plenty of support this time around, while another of the 1978 placed horses, Drumroan, returned to Aintree after a below-average campaign.

David Goulding, who had agonisingly missed out on the ride on Lucius twelve months before, was hoping for compensation this time aboard Rambling Artist. The horse was certainly not without a chance, and was listed at 16/1 having recently run a race of interesting potential behind Alverton at Haydock Park.

Among the other newcomers who seemed to be live Grand National contenders were Rubstic, Rough And Tumble and Kick On. Rubstic hailed from Scotland and arrived for the race with a reputation for having reserves of stamina, having twice finished second in the Scottish Grand National and never once suffered a racing fall. Fred Winter's entry, Rough And Tumble, gave jockey John Francome a serious chance of landing his first Grand National, while Kick On was another that the extreme distance of the race was unlikely to affect, as the horse had won the Midlands Grand National the previous April.

With the fate of the thirty-four runners about to be revealed, the huge crowd of 66,000 cheered in anticipation as the race came under starter's orders. It was Bob Champion who led the frantic charge to the first fence on Purdo and he sailed over without incident. Not so fortunate were Double Negative, Sandwilan, Wayward Scot and Vindicate, who all crashed out of the action.

Purdo kept up his lead from Jenny Pitman's runner Artistic Prince, together with Zongalero, Drumroan, Rubstic, Kick On and Ben Nevis, and the next four fences passed without claiming any more fallers as they faced up to Becher's Brook for the first time.

Taking the mighty fence in the lead, it was Purdo's turn to make an exit, while 100/1 shot Oskard also fell out of contention. At this stage, Alverton's jumping was holding up well and the Gold Cup winner was travelling within himself just behind the leaders, who were now headed by the red and white colours of Zongalero.

As they jumped the Canal Turn, a pattern was starting to emerge in front as Zongalero led from Rubstic and Alverton, but Tommy Carmody's National dream was over as he parted company with Sandpit, and at the tenth, Drumroan too was out of the race.

As the field came back across the Melling Road and on to the racecourse, a pair of loose horses, Oskard and Double Negative, were beginning to make a nuisance of themselves, and as the field progressed to the much-feared Chair, the troublesome duo were still harassing the leaders.

The Swiss-owned horse Wagner, together with Zongalero and Rubstic, jumped the Chair without incident in the lead, but behind them, major destruction was about to commence. Narrowly missing the race favourite Alverton, the loose horses tore straight along the slim take-off path of the runners, colliding with the chasing group and causing complete chaos. In the aftermath, Rambling Artist, Ben Nevis, No Gypsy, Alpenstock, Kick On, Cartwright and Godfrey Secundus had been brought down, The Champ had fallen, and tragically, Kintai had broken his back in the melée and had to be put down.

With the field decimated, it was Wagner who led on to the second lap, followed by Zongalero, Rubstic, Alverton, Rough And Tumble, Artistic Prince, Lord Browndodd and Coolishall.

It was noticeable how easily Alverton was going, and although he made a small error at the twentieth, it was not enough to stop him in his tracks and favourite backers were beginning to count their money already, as the runners approached Becher's again.

But in a cruel twist, Alverton altered his stride pattern running to the fence and never got back in to rhythm. In one of the saddest moments in recent Grand National history, the Gold Cup hero smashed in to the fence chest-first, giving himself no chance of a recovery, and he plummeted to the ground and broke his neck.

As the remainder of the runners left the dark scene at Becher's, Lord Browndodd was the next to depart the race when Andy Turnell pulled him up at the Canal Turn with blood coming from the horse's nose, while Mr Snowman was also pulled up, having been remounted following a fall at Becher's.

Out in front, it was still Wagner, Zongalero, Rubstic and Rough And Tumble, while The Pilgarlic was starting to make ground on the leaders, but Coolishall came to grief when still in contention at the twenty-seventh.

At the second last, John Francome had sent Rough And Tumble through on the inside to take the lead from Rubstic on the outside with Nicky Henderson's chaser Zongalero between the pair. The Pilgarlic was still in touch but his challenge was beginning to wither while Wagner had also been left behind as the pace quickened.

Sensing a first National victory, Francome urged Rough And Tumble on jumping the last, and although his mount responded gamely, Rubstic and Zongalero were staying on stronger. By the elbow, the two of them had collared Rough And Tumble and had begun their own private battle to the line.

Inside the final furlong, Maurice Barnes on Rubstic vigorously cajoled his horse in front and the ten-year-old fought bravely to edge his sheepskin noseband clear and was able to deny Zongalero by a length and a half. Having given his all, Rough And Tumble came home behind the principals in third with The Pilgarlic registering another fine run in fourth.

Bob Davies was narrowly denied another win after Lucius the year before, but the bravery of his horse Zongalero was evident after it emerged he had returned lame.

Most saddened of all jockeys though was Jonjo O'Neill after the tragic demise of Alverton and the distraught rider was unable to speak for a long time after the race, such was the severity of his loss. With Kintai also a fatality after the drama at the Chair, the National inevitably came in for a great deal of finger pointing.

For Rubstic and his connections though, it was a day to remember. The horse had become the first ever winner to be trained in Scotland and was the crowning moment in the training career of John Leadbetter. Leadbetter had only taken out a permit in 1975 and his first season had yielded just one winner.

Rubstic himself had been seriously ill two years previously, and had almost died through dehydration. The gallant horse had recovered, though, and now presented his owner John Douglas with jump racing's most famous prize after a courageous display of staying power and fighting spirit.

HORSE/FATE	AGE/WEIGHT	JOCKEY	ODDS
1st RUBSTIC	10.10-0	M. BARNES	25/1
2nd ZONGALERO	9.10-5	B.R. DAVIES	20/1
3rd ROUGH AND TUMBLE	9.10-7	J. FRANCOME	14/1
4th THE PILGARLIC	11.10-1	R.R. EVANS	16/1
5th Wagner	9.10-0	R. Lamb	50/1
6th Royal Frolic	10.11-0	J. Burke	25/1
7th Prime Justice	9.10-0	A.K. Taylor	200/1
Ben Nevis - *Brought Down*	11.11-2	Mr C. Fenwick	14/1
Alverton - *Fell*	9.10-13	J.J. O'Neill	13/2
The Champ - *Fell*	11.10-12	W. Smith	25/1
Purdo - *Fell*	8.10-12	R. Champion	25/1
Mr Snowman - *Fell*	10.10-9	G. Thorner	10/1
Sandpit - *Fell*	9.10-7	T. Carmody	22/1
Wayward Scot - *Fell*	10.10-7	R.F. Davies	100/1
Rambling Artist - *Brought Down*	9.10-6	D. Goulding	16/1
Drumroan - *Fell*	11.10-4	G. Newman	20/1
Godfrey Secundus - *Brought Down*	9.10-3	C. Tinkler	25/1
Coolishall - *Fell*	10.10-2	A. Webber	12/1
Double Negative - *Fell*	9.10-5	Mr E. Woods	66/1
Artistic Prince - *Fell*	8.10-3	P. Blacker	25/1
Lord Browndodd - *Pulled Up*	11.10-3	A. Turnell	25/1
Red Earl - *Pulled Up*	10.10-0	H.J. Evans	50/1
Kintai - *Brought Down*	10.10-0	B. Smart	100/1
No Gypsy - *Brought Down*	10.10-1	J. Suthern	66/1
Churchtown Boy - *Brought Down*	12.10-0	M. Salaman	25/1
Dromore - *Pulled Up*	11.10-10	Mr P. Duggan	50/1
Kick On - *Brought Down*	12.10-0	R. Hyett	50/1
Flitgrove - *Pulled Up*	8.10-1	R. Linley	50/1
Oskard - *Fell*	10.10-0	M. Blackshaw	100/1
Alpenstock - *Brought Down*	12.10-0	Mr D. Gray	100/1
Brown Admiral - *Unseated Rider*	10.10-0	S. Morshead	100/1
Sandwilan - *Fell*	11.10-0	Mrs J. Hembrow	100/1
Vindicate - *Fell*	12.11-8	Mr A. O'Connell	200/1
Cartwright - *Brought Down*	10.10-0	A. Phillips	200/1

1980
BEN NEVIS

The opening Grand National of the 1980s saw *The Sun* newspaper sponsor the race for the first time, so it was with a sense of irony that their association with the event was welcomed by relentless rain leading up to the race, resulting in testing and stamina-sapping conditions for the contestants. Originally, Man Alive was to run as joint top-weight along with Royal Frolic, but the grey horse, winner of the Mackeson Gold Cup earlier in the season, was withdrawn on the morning of the race due to the state of the ground, together with Wagner, fifth in the race the year before.

As a result, the betting market was dominated by the first three to finish in 1979, Rubstic, Zongalero and Rough And Tumble. Of the trio, the majority of the money came for Rubstic, as he looked to follow Red Rum's achievement of recording back-to-back victories. Even though he had 11lb more to carry than the previous season, Rubstic had won his last two races and, remarkably, had never fallen in a race. With Maurice Barnes again in the saddle, the horse's chance was obvious, and his price of 8/1 reflected that. Of Rubstic's victims last season, Zongalero now had a new jockey in Steve Smith-Eccles, who was having his first ride in the Grand National, while John Francome was again booked to ride Rough And Tumble, although the horse had not won a race for sixteen months. Both horses started at 11/1.

Dissecting the three returnees in the market was a strongly-fancied newcomer in nine-year-old Jer. Partnered at Aintree by another first-timer in Phil Tuck, Jer had won three of his last six races, including the Great Yorkshire Chase, where he had beaten Rubstic, and had been second on his latest start. At 10/1, the horse received warm support on the day. After his unpleasant experience on Alverton twelve months ago, Jonjo O'Neill was hoping for better luck on Fred Rimell's latest Aintree challenger, Another Dolly. Although the horse had not won for some time, Another Dolly could offer the excuse of suffering from leg troubles and his Grand National chances had increased after finishing a strong second in the recent Queen Mother Champion Chase at Cheltenham. With the possibility of becoming an amazing fifth National winner for Rimell, Another Dolly had grabbed a lot of attention in the weeks leading up to the race and was backed down from 66/1 to a starting price of 12/1.

Well fancied when brought down at the Chair in 1979, Ben Nevis was not nearly as strongly considered on this occasion. Again ridden by American amateur Charlie Fenwick, the horse had yet to win a race since joining Tim Forster, and with a history of dislike for soft ground, the recent rain had apparently ruined any chance he may have had. It was with a great deal of pessimism from connections that he took his place in the field. Of the others to line up, former Gold Cup winner Royal Frolic had regained some form during the season with a pair of wins, while despite having poor form outside Aintree, big race specialist The Pilgarlic was expected to give a good account of himself. With conditions underfoot resulting in a sensibly-paced start to the race, it was clear that only the most determined and hardy of competitors were going to complete the challenge that lay before them. It was another horse new to the event that led his twenty-nine rivals to the first fence, in the form of Delmoss, and the action quickly brought around a number of casualties, with Salkeld and

Mannyboy departing at the opening obstacle. Jer's chances evaporated with a fall at the big ditch, where the Aintree stalwart Churchtown Boy was also brought down. Coolishall was the next to depart a fence later when he unseated his rider with a broken iron.

Out in front and jumping extravagantly, Delmoss led the charge down to Becher's Brook, joined by Rubstic, So And So, Zongalero, Levanka and Sandwilan, ridden by Mrs Jenny Hembrow. The gallop had increased dramatically by this point and the pace, together with the famous Becher's drop, was enough to catch out So And So, who crumpled on landing, while towards the rear, Jonjo O'Neill again saw his hopes dashed at Becher's as Another Dolly took an ugly fall. Last of all over the fence was Ben Nevis, seemingly going nowhere on the rain-soaked ground. By the time the field had returned on to the racecourse, Delmoss had carved out a handy lead over Rubstic, Levanka, Sandwilan, Kininvie and Rough And Tumble, while slowly but surely, Ben Nevis began to weave his way through the pack. As Delmoss flew the Chair accompanied by a loose horse, there appeared no danger of a repeat of the previous year's drama. However, a shock of different proportions took place as Rubstic, miscalculating the gaping ditch before the fence, clouted the top of the Chair and succumbed to his first-ever fall, resulting in disbelieving groans from the crowd.

With the gallop set by Delmoss beginning to take its toll on many in the field, the runners were quickly being whittled down as the race went on. The Vinter pulled up rather than begin another circuit and Even Up refused soon after. The nineteenth claimed Casamayor and Drumroan, with Prince Rock, Sandwilan, Godfrey Secundus and Kininvie all deciding enough was enough, while Zongalero bowed out totally exhausted a fence later.

With the numbers now greatly depleted, it was Delmoss and Ben Nevis who disputed the lead and the two were well clear as they faced up to Becher's again. Here, Delmoss made a terrible mistake and came crashing down, and behind the front two, Three To One suffered a nearly identical fall. This left Ben Nevis with a strong advantage at the twenty-third, and with only a small band of competitors remaining, including Rough And Tumble, The Pilgarlic and Royal Stuart, American hopes were suddenly as wide as the Atlantic Ocean.

Over the last fences, none of the survivors could get close enough to Ben Nevis to strike a blow, and although Rough And Tumble was within four lengths of the leader at the last, he was tiring while Ben Nevis proceeded to gallop clear in fine style, drawing even further away as he passed the elbow, and he crossed the line with American applause ringing in his ears, a comfortable twenty-length winner. In what was the slowest race since 1955, only four horses managed to complete the war of attrition, with the front two followed home by The Pilgarlic and finally the New Zealand-bred Royal Stuart, with Philip Blacker on board.

The official time was of no concern to the jubilant Ben Nevis team, as the twelve-year-old was led triumphantly in to the famed winner's enclosure. In victory, Ben Nevis had achieved the aim that was set for him when leaving his owner, Mr Red C. Stewart Jnr, in America eighteen months previously. Mr Charlie Fenwick, a thirty-two-year-old banker from Baltimore and son-in-law of the owner, had given the horse a fabulous ride, having only arrived in England two days before the National. For Ben Nevis, his goal had been met, and he had proven himself a gutsy, whole-hearted performer, while trainer Tim Forster, now a two-time winner of the race, expressed his opinion and desire that the brave hero would now be given a well-earned retirement.

HORSE/FATE	AGE/WEIGHT	JOCKEY	ODDS
1st **BEN NEVIS**	**12.10-12**	**MR C. FENWICK**	**40/1**
2nd **ROUGH AND TUMBLE**	**10.10-11**	**J. FRANCOME**	**11/1**
3rd **THE PILGARLIC**	**12.10-4**	**R. HYETT**	**33/1**
4th **ROYAL STUART**	**9.10-10**	**P. BLACKER**	**20/1**
Royal Frolic - *Refused*	11.11-4	J. Burke	16/1
Price Rock - *Refused*	12.11-0	T. Carmody	12/1
Zongalero - *Refused*	10.10-13	S. Smith-Eccles	11/1
Casamayor - *Fell*	10.10-12	J. King	50/1
Rubstic - *Fell*	11.10-11	M. Barnes	8/1
Another Dolly - *Fell*	10.10-10	J.J. O'Neill	12/1
So And So - *Fell*	11.10-10	R. Linley	28/1
Flashy Boy - *Fell*	12.10-8	C. Grant	50/1
The Vinter - *Pulled Up*	9.10-8	B.R. Davies	16/1
Coolishall - *Unseated Rider*	11.10-10	Mr B. Munro-Wilson	40/1
Even Up - *Refused*	13.10-6	A. Webber	50/1
Our Greenwood - *Fell*	12.11-6	Mr A. O'Connell	100/1
Jimmy Miff - *Fell*	8.10-5	A. Brown	50/1
Drumroan - *Fell*	12.10-5	T. McGivern	22/1
Jer - *Fell*	9.10-4	P. Tuck	10/1
Levanka - *Pulled Up*	11.10-4	F. Berry	100/1
Delmoss - *Fell*	10.10-2	G. Newman	25/1
Mannyboy - *Unseated Rider*	10.10-2	R. Rowe	33/1
Salkeld - *Fell*	8.10-0	C. Hawkins	20/1
Dromore - *Pulled Up*	12.10-8	Mr P. Duggan	100/1
Churchtown Boy - *Brought Down*	13.10-0	A. Turnell	50/1
Godfrey Secundus - *Pulled Up*	10.10-0	S. Morshead	20/1
Three To One - *Fell*	9.10-2	Mr T.G. Dun	25/1
Sandwilan - *Pulled Up*	12.10-0	Mrs J. Hembrow	100/1
Kininvie - *Pulled Up*	11.10-0	J. Williams	100/1
Rathlek - *Refused*	10.10-0	P. Barton	35/1

1981
ALDANITI

Not a soul present at Aintree for the Grand National in 1981 was unaware of the remarkable path that had led one of the competing partnerships to the famous event. Seldom, if ever, could a story be more suitable for a fairytale ending than the defiant and often distressing episode that was portrayed by Bob Champion and his mount, Aldaniti.

Champion was a veteran jockey who first rode in the National in 1971. Having not enjoyed much luck in the race and never finishing any higher than sixth place, the rider had partnered Purdo, who fell early on in the 1979 contest. A few months later, Champion was catastrophically diagnosed with cancer, and what lay ahead of him was a battle far more testing than any of the enormous Aintree fences he had encountered before.

For his part, the highly-talented Aldaniti had suffered a series of career-threatening leg injuries that would have left the majority of horses afflicted as invalids, and it was after the most recent recurrence of the problem in November 1979, that his trainer, Josh Gifford, had sent the horse back to the home of his owner, Mr Nick Embiricos, where he was eased back to fitness with road-walking and trotting, before being returned to Gifford's yard.

Courageously, and to the absolute delight of everyone, Champion defeated his dreaded illness, often inspired in his recovery by the thought of partnering his old friend Aldaniti in the ultimate horserace, the Grand National. The horse had also responded admirably to the care and attention he had received, and with Champion determined to make his dream a reality, the two, against all the odds, were reunited for a trial race at Ascot in February, which they won convincingly.

Although during his chasing career Aldaniti had been third in a Cheltenham Gold Cup and second in a Scottish Grand National, just one race after a very long lay off was hardly the ideal preparation for the perils and sheer distance the National would present. Even so, with a momentous wave of public support and a great deal of hope, the pairing began their Aintree assault as 10/1 second favourites.

The opposition was incredibly strong and plentiful, with one horse in particular possessing the necessary form over the daunting Aintree fences to attract significant interest. The horse was Spartan Missile, owned, trained and bred by his fifty-four-year old jockey Mr John Thorne. A hunter-chaser, Spartan Missile had twice won the Foxhunter's Chase at Aintree and had proved that he belonged in top class company when finishing fourth in the recent Cheltenham Gold Cup. The Grand National would be only the second time that Spartan Missile would be contesting a handicap race, with the previous occasion seeing him finish second in the 1978 Whitbread Gold Cup. Despite suffering a worrying fall at Haydock Park three runs prior to the National, Spartan Missile rightly held a favourite's chance at 8/1. Aintree veterans Rubstic and Zongalero were both back at the National after failing to get round the year before. Rubstic had won a good staying contest at Doncaster under a big weight recently, but Zongalero had disappointingly pulled up on his last two starts.

Top weight was the high-class eleven-year-old Royal Mail. Among his notable achievements were capturing the previous season's Whitbread Gold Cup and finishing second to Alverton in the 1979 Cheltenham Gold Cup. Philip Blacker took the mount on the 16/1 shot.

A top-quality field also contained Senator Maclacury, Royal Exile and Royal Stuart. Senator Maclacury was the big hope of Ireland and was a first National runner for trainer Jonjo Walsh. Small in appearance, Senator Maclacury had proved his liking for long distances when claiming the Punchestown National Trial earlier in the season. Royal Exile was ridden by youngster Ben De Haan for trainer Fred Winter and arrived in winning form, while the consistent Royal Stuart was looking to improve on the fourth place he had registered in 1980.

With the eyes of the world fixed on the thirty-nine runners, the sun lit up the April afternoon to glorious effect and as they hurtled towards the first fence, it was outsider Kininvie who was first to show and landed over the obstacle safely. Barney Maclyvie and Another Captain were the first to exit the contest, and Aldaniti almost ruined all his hard work with a mistake straight away.

Surviving the blunder, he and Champion continued at the back of the field as Carrow Boy joined Kininvie up front. The fourth fence, normally an incident-free obstacle, was this time to be the downfall of Delmoss, Kilkilwell, Chumson and Bryan Boru, but the rest of the runners kept their poise and marched on to Becher's Brook.

The leading group at the giant fence were Tenecoon, Carrow Boy, Lord Gulliver, Kininvie and Choral Festival, and the usual booby-trap on the landing side failed to claim any victims on this occasion. However, further pitfalls lay in store and those next to succumb were Another Prospect at the Canal Turn, Carrow Boy when leading at the tenth, and Tenecoon a fence later.

Racing towards the thirteenth fence, Aldaniti began to rouse the spirits of his followers as he started to show his white face on the outside of the current leader, Zongalero, but the fence caught out Lord Gulliver, and as the field went on to clear the Chair to the roar of the crowd, there were plenty still in the hunt for glory.

Having been carefully guided round the first circuit in expert fashion, Aldaniti now jumped to the head of affairs at the seventeenth, soaring over each new obstacle to belie his former troubles. The mare Kylogue Lady departed here and the field soon became strung out as Champion called the shots out in front.

Aldaniti was sticking to the inside as they met the big ditch, followed closely by Rubstic and Pacify, while Royal Stuart was making ominous progress until he made a bad blunder which knocked him back, and a fence later, Hywel Davies was unseated from the horse with his leathers broken.

With the runners well spaced out, Aldaniti proudly approached Becher's with a slim advantage from Rubstic, Pacify and the top weight Royal Mail, but while his fellow leaders cleared the fence safely, Pacify crumbled on landing when travelling

A magical end to the fairytale as Bob Champion and Aldaniti hold off the challenge of Spartan Missile and veteran rider John Thorne.

nicely. Then came a gap back to Three To One, Senator Maclacury, Spartan Missile, Royal Exile, Might Be and Rathlek, and a winner from further back than this group would have been unthinkable.

Again the outlook of the race changed as they jumped the Canal Turn, with Aldaniti and Royal Mail surging clear of former winner Rubstic, who simply could not keep up with the pace. The two leaders soon found themselves involved in a private duel and by the time they arrived at two from home, Aldaniti still had the edge. Looming as a real threat to the leader, Royal Mail made a shocking mistake which almost sent Philip Blacker to the floor, and now the prospect of Aldaniti winning appeared to be a likely one.

Although a slow jump at the last briefly had his supporters worried, Aldaniti was quickly away, with Royal Mail struggling now to respond to the challenge. Just as it seemed that the dream result was about to be realised, Spartan Missile, who had been making relentless progress since rounding the final turn, suddenly emerged as a potential destroyer of the romantic ending. Driven along in inspired style by John Thorne, the favourite flashed past Royal Mail at the elbow and soon had Aldaniti in his sights.

However, such was the bravery and staying power of Aldaniti that he again responded to Champion's urgings and strode home to win by four lengths to the thunderous and emotional delight of the crowd. Obviously realising the magnitude of what had just been achieved, Thorne was the first to congratulate his conqueror in a genuine example of true sportsmanship.

Filling the minor places were the brave Royal Mail and the fast-finishing Three To One, with Ireland's plucky Senator Maclacury in fifth.

Predicting a winning effort from Spartan Missile in 1982, Thorne stated that he hoped to ride his horse again and felt that he had lost the race on this occasion after being hampered at the Canal turn, while another disappointed jockey was Hywel Davies, who considered Royal Stuart to be cruising sweetly when he made his exit.

Not lost in the whirlwind of celebrations that joyfully followed was the magnificent training feat pulled off by Josh Gifford, with a horse whose career had looked doomed at one stage. Unlucky not to win the 1967 Grand National as a jockey on Honey End, Gifford also designated a large share of credit to the horse's owners, Mr and Mrs Embiricos, for their part in Aldaniti's recovery and also their willingness to run him in the Grand National. Having sadly lost their good horse Stonepark over the big fences two days before, it was only after a rethink and probable honour to Champion that Aldaniti finally took his place in the field.

But the day without doubt belonged to the gallant winning horse and jockey who had met the Aintree challenge with the same dedication and strength that they had shown in their previous battles in life. On a day where hope was handed out to thousands through their accomplishments, the 1981 victors could truly be described as heroes.

HORSE/FATE	AGE/WEIGHT	JOCKEY	ODDS
1st **ALDANITI**	11.10-13	R. CHAMPION	10/1
2nd **SPARTAN MISSILE**	9.11-5	MR M.J. THORNE	8/1*
3rd **ROYAL MAIL**	11.11-7	P. BLACKER	16/1
4th **THREE TO ONE**	10.10-3	MR T.G. DUN	33/1
5th Senator Maclacury	7.10-12	J. Burke	20/1
6th Royal Exile	12.10-0	B. De Haan	16/1
7th Rubstic	12.10-7	M. Barnes	11/1
8th Coolishall	12.10-3	W. Smith	25/1
9th Rathlek	11.10-1	P. Barton	50/1
10th So	12.10-8	J. Francome	40/1
11th Sebastian V	13.10-2	R. Lamb	33/1
12th Cheers	9.10-0	P. Scudamore	20/1
Carrow Boy - *Fell*	9.11-6	G. Newman	33/1
Chumson - *Fell*	10.11-7	Mr A. O'Connell	50/1
Zongalero - *Fell*	11.10-11	S. Smith-Eccles	14/1
Barney Maclyvie - *Fell*	10.10-8	M. Lynch	33/1
The Vintner - *Refused*	10.10-8	C. Grant	20/1
Martinstown - *Fell*	9.10-7	Mr M. Batters	33/1
Casamayor - *Refused*	11.10-6	Mr P .Webber	100/1
Kilkilwell - *Fell*	9.10-6	N. Madden	33/1
Another Prospect - *Fell*	9.10-8	M.A.J. Wilson	40/1
Royal Stuart - *Unseated Rider*	10.10-2	H. Davies	16/1
Delmoss - *Fell*	11.10-1	F. Berry	50/1
Drumroan - *Fell*	13.10-6	Mr M. Graffe	50/1
Kylogue Lady - *Fell*	9.10-0	T. Quinn	100/1
Lord Gulliver - *Fell*	8.10-0	C. Brown	50/1
Might Be - *Fell*	10.10-0	A. Webber	50/1
Bryan Boru - *Refused*	10.10-0	Mr J. Carden	100/1
Pacify - *Fell*	11.10-0	S. Jobar	50/1
Another Captain - *Fell*	9.10-0	C. Hawkins	40/1
Tenecoon - *Fell*	12.10-0	C. Mann	100/1
My Friendly Cousin - *Pulled Up*	11.10-2	A. Brown	100/1
Son And Heir - *Refused*	11.10-0	S. Morshead	100/1
Dromore - *Refused*	13.10-8	Mr P. Duggan	100/1
Choral Festival - *Fell*	10.10-2	Mr M.J. Low	66/1
No Gypsy - *Fell*	12.10-0	J. Suthern	100/1
Three Of Diamonds - *Fell*	9.10-4	P. Leach	100/1
Kininvie - *Fell*	12.10-0	P. Hobbs	100/1
Deiopia - *Refused*	10.10-0	Mrs L. Sheedy	100/1

1982
GRITTAR

A shadowy covering of sadness accompanied the 1982 Grand National. John Thorne, a noble runner-up the year before on Spartan Missile, had tragically lost his life following a fall in a point-to-point race just weeks prior to the race.

With his loss a blow to the world of racing, further problems, although incomparable in reality, lay ahead for the National. Now in the final year of the Ladbrokes agreement, Bill Davies had decided to price the course at £7 million, a huge increase on his original purchase. It was the Jockey Club who then responded by officially launching an appeal for the money to save the race. The deadline was to be November that year, and failure to raise the required funds would again result in the fear that there would be no more Grand Nationals at Aintree.

It was to be another amateur that would have the mount on the big race favourite this time. Mr Dick Saunders, who was forty-eight-years old, had the responsibility of guiding round the fine-jumping nine-year-old Grittar. Like his late friend Thorne's horse Spartan Missile, Grittar was also a hunter-chaser and he had taken both the Cheltenham and Aintree Foxhunter Chases the previous season. After an encouraging sixth place in the recent

Grittar, seen here winning at Cheltenham, comfortably won the National in 1982.

Cheltenham Gold Cup, Grittar started at 7/1 for his permit-holding Leicestershire trainer, Mr Frank Gilman.

Having masterfully claimed his cherished Grand National crown the year before, Bob Champion was back with Aldaniti to try and repeat the success. Now a twelve-year-old, Aldaniti had finished unplaced on his two runs during the season and had to shoulder an extra 10lb this time around. His most recent run at Haydock Park, however, had given his supporters some cause for optimism, and Josh Gifford's charge started at 12/1.

More fancied than last year's winner, though one of his victims on that occasion, was Royal Mail. Having run a superb race at Aintree in 1981, Royal Mail had been given a light campaign and he arrived for the National having won well at Doncaster in March. Besides his heavily-backed top weight, trainer Stan Mellor was also represented by Cold Spell and Aintree old-hand Royal Stuart.

Three To One had finished brightly in the previous Grand National, and his form prior to Aintree on this occasion was encouraging. Having been successful at Hexham last time out, Three To One was strongly considered to give Ken Oliver a National winner – the trainer having managed second places in the 1960s through Wyndburgh and Moidore's Token.

A host of interesting newcomers to the National included Peter Scot, Tragus, Loving Words, Again The Same and Deep Gale. At 16/1, Peter Scot was a former winner of the Welsh Grand National and the mount of Paul Barton had only fallen once in thirty-four races. Peter Scudamore's bold-jumping ride Tragus took his place in the line-up on the back of two good wins, while the tough-staying, grey horse Loving Words had shown a liking for extreme distances when landing a four-miler at Warwick earlier in the season. Although suffering an interrupted preparation, Again The Same presented Jonjo O'Neill with a solid chance of finally completing the National course and had run with promise at Ascot in March, while Deep Gale ran in the colours of major Irish punter J.P. McManus.

The thirty-nine runners who gathered at the start featured two hopeful female riders. Miss Charlotte Brew partnered her mother's horse, Martinstown, while Mrs Geraldine Rees got her opportunity aboard 66/1 outsider Cheers.

Led by the trail-blazing front-runner Delmoss, the big field, unusually strung out at such an early stage, charged seemingly out of control towards the first fence at a tremendous pace. With such a fierce gallop, the carnage that took place was inevitable. Disputing the lead with Delmoss as they rose at the first, Deep Gale was the first to go as the horse crashed face-first in to the turf. An excess of spectacular falls followed behind, including the grey Man Alive, who skidded for a number of yards before finally dislodging Andy Turnell. There would be no glittering conclusion on this occasion for last year's winner, as Aldaniti also capsized towards the back of the pack. In what amounted to the highest number of fallers at the first since 1951 (when twelve went), a total of ten horses departed at the first obstacle – Mullacurry, Three To One, Rambling Jack, Jimmy Miff, Cold Spell, Artistic Prince and Rathlek being the others to go.

With the big ditch claiming another four runners, the field was already drastically depleted as they made for Becher's Brook. With the leading group consisting of Delmoss, Carrow Boy, Saint Fillans and Grittar, the famous obstacle was to catch out another unlucky quartet. A rare tumble from Peter Scot was matched by that of another top fancy, Royal Mail.

With The Vintner and Choral Festival unseating their riders and Again The Same's mistake enough to continue O'Neill's dreadful luck at the fence, over half the field were out of the race by the Canal Turn.

Settling down in to some sort of normality, Delmoss led the sparse band of survivors back on to the racecourse and on to the thirteenth. Severely interfered with by the rider-less Jimmy Miff approaching the fence, jockey Bill Smith performed a miracle to guide Delmoss over safely, albeit in a wild, unconventional manner. But unlike many others, the partnership were still in the race, and leading clearly from Carrow Boy, Saint Fillans and Good Prospect, Delmoss took them on over the Chair, the Water and out for another circuit.

With the leader unable to keep up such a hectic pace, Carrow Boy was soon able to close Delmoss down and take up the running from Saint Fillans, Grittar, Loving Words, Tragus and Hard Outlook, and from here on in, these would be the major players.

It was at Becher's second time that the final pattern of the race emerged. Saint Fillans made a bad blunder, and this allowed Grittar to overtake Phil Tuck's mount and race on into the lead at the twenty-third fence.

Grittar had now assumed complete command and the favourite began a relentless gallop out in the country for the final time, jumping fluently and confidently down the inside of the track. His progress was made even more straightforward when Saint Fillans and Carrow Boy crashed out four from home, causing Loving Words to swerve violently and unship jockey Richard Hoare.

With just Hard Outlook now remaining to chase the favourite over the last few fences, Grittar was showing no signs of stopping.

Hard Outlook got to within four lengths at the second last, but even though Grittar plunged through the top of the final flight, he kept his gallop going strongly and went well clear at the elbow.

Passing the post as one of the most comfortable winners of recent times, the 11st 5lb on his back had proved a meagre burden for the excellent winner. Hard Outlook had run a smashing first Grand National and came home fifteen lengths behind the winner. The connections of Loving Words were left to ponder what might have been as the grey horse, remounted after the drama four out, made up a tremendous amount of ground in the closing stages to deny the tearaway Delmoss third place.

Some time later, a milestone was reached as an exhausted-looking Cheers, roared on by the crowd and coaxed home over the last few fences by amateur Pat O'Connor on Three Of Diamonds, carried Geraldine Rees to the finish, enabling her to become the first female rider to complete the great race.

At forty-eight, Saunders had become the oldest rider to win the race and graciously pinned all the glory on his majestic horse. As he had vowed to do all along, the amateur jockey then announced he would be retiring from race riding for good.

Mr Frank Gilman also made history by becoming the first permit holder to train a National winner. In Grittar, he had an exceptional horse, and one who would be young enough to return to Aintree in upcoming years to contest, as so many hoped, future Grand Nationals.

HORSE/FATE	AGE/WEIGHT	JOCKEY	ODDS
1st **GRITTAR**	9.11-5	MR C.R. SAUNDERS	7/1*
2nd **HARD OUTLOOK**	11.10-1	A. WEBBER	50/1
3rd **LOVING WORDS**	9.10-11	R. HOARE - *Remount*	16/1
4th **DELMOSS**	12.10-3	W. SMITH	50/1
5th Current Gold	11.10-8	N. Doughty	25/1
6th Tragus	10.11-4	P. Scudamore	14/1
7th Three Of Diamonds	10.10-7	Mr P. O'Connor	100/1
8th Cheers	10.10-0	Mrs Geraldine Rees	66/1
Royal Mail - *Fell*	12.11-10	B.R. Davies	17/2
Aldaniti - *Fell*	12.11-9	R. Champion	12/1
Again The Same - *Pulled Up*	9.11-8	J.J. O'Neill	16/1
Carrow Boy - *Fell*	10.11-7	G. Newman	40/1
Peter Scot - *Fell*	11.11-5	P. Barton	16/1
Deep Gale - *Fell*	9.11-2	T.J. Ryan	22/1
Rambling Jack - *Fell*	11.11-1	T.G. Dun	16/1
Man Alive - *Fell*	11.11-0	A. Turnell	33/1
Mullacurry - *Fell*	10.10-12	Mr T.J. Taafe	16/1
Rolls Rambler - *Refused*	11.10-12	Mr A.J. Wilson	20/1
Saint Fillans - *Fell*	8.10-11	P. Tuck	33/1
Good Prospect - *Refused*	13.10-12	R. Linley	50/1
Gandy VI - *Fell*	13.10-8	N. Madden	50/1
Old Society - *Fell*	8.10-8	P. Walsh	33/1
Rough And Tumble - *Refused*	12.10-8	J. Francome	16/1
The Vintner - *Unseated Rider*	11.10-7	Mr D. Browne	50/1
Royal Stuart - *Brought Down*	11.10-4	Mr D. Gray	40/1
Martinstown - *Unseated Rider*	10.10.3	Miss Charlotte Brew	100/1
Three To One - *Fell*	11.10-3	R. Lamb	12/1
Sun Lion - *Fell*	12.10-3	S. Smith-Eccles	50/1
Tiepolino - *Refused*	10.10-4	H. Davies	50/1
Coolishall - *Fell*	13.10-3	R. Barry	33/1
Senator Maclacury - *Fell*	8.10-0	P. Kiely	20/1
Artistic Prince - *Fell*	11.10-0	C. Brown	50/1
Jimmy Miff - *Fell*	10.10-1	Mr M. Williams	50/1
Monty Python - *Refused*	10.10-0	B.De Haan	66/1
Cold Spell - *Brought Down*	10.10-0	S. Jobar	40/1
This Way - *Fell*	11.10-2	C. Candy	100/1
Choral Festival - *Unseated Rider*	11.10-4	Mr.M.Low	100/1
Deermount - *Fell*	8.10-0	J.P. Byrne	100/1
Rathlek - *Fell*	12.10-12	Mr J. Carden	100/1

1983
CORBIERE

After Mrs Geraldine Rees had made the breakthrough for female jockeys in the previous season's race, the 1983 Grand National – thankfully going ahead after the race appeal deadline was put back to later in the year – saw three lady trainers with strongly fancied runners. Each of Jenny Pitman, Helen Hamilton and Mercy Rimell had reason to believe that this could be the year for them to make history.

The favourite though, just as in 1982, was the outstanding reigning champion Grittar. The top weight, with 7lb more to carry this time, had not had an ideal preparation for the race, and it was by trainer Frank Gilman's own admission that the horse probably needed one more warm-up run. Even so, the horse's previous exploits over the massive fences had been exceptional and, after a close second on his most recent run at Nottingham, Grittar attracted a wealth of public interest and started with a favourite's chance at 6/1.

With the ground for the 1983 race on the soft side, a horse that captured a great deal of attention was National first-timer Bonum Omen. With his last three runs all victorious ones, the horse had shown a love for long-distance slogs in the mud, and had recorded marathon wins at Cheltenham and Warwick. His trainer, Fulke Walwyn, was confident too that the recent wet weather would be of no detriment to Bonum Omen, instead expecting the horse to relish the Aintree conditions. With an ideal racing weight to boot, the newcomer was listed second in the market at 13/2.

Although having a reputation as a sometimes sketchy jumper, having on several occasions made fencing errors in his native Ireland, Michael Cunningham's runner Greasepaint was well fancied, having won two of his last three races. The horse had attracted a lot of interest following a recent win at Cheltenham and had only 10st 7lb to carry at Aintree. Greasepaint had also proven his resilience and toughness during the season when, after suffering a fall at Leopardstown in December, he responded to win at Punchestown two days later.

Of the six runners trained by female trainers, Jenny Pitman saddled three of them, including outsiders Artistic Prince and Monty Python. But it was the eight-year-old chestnut Corbiere who was the most heavily supported of the trio. The horse had shown grit and endurance when beating Mercy Rimell's National hope Pilot Officer to win the season's Welsh Grand National, and had also run with promise at Cheltenham on his last outing. With the going at Aintree to Corbiere's liking, the 13/1 chance was expected to deliver a bold display on his Grand National debut.

Another of Corbiere's victims in the Welsh National was the Helen Hamilton-trained Peaty Sandy. The horse appreciated soft ground and had enjoyed a season of fine consistency with a recent win a Kelso following an excellent run behind the eminent Cheltenham Gold Cup second, Captain John. A price of 12/1 illustrated the horse's distinct chance. Other notable runners in a huge field included Spartan Missile, Mid Day Gun, Beacon Time and King Spruce. The heavily-weighted Spartan Missile was now

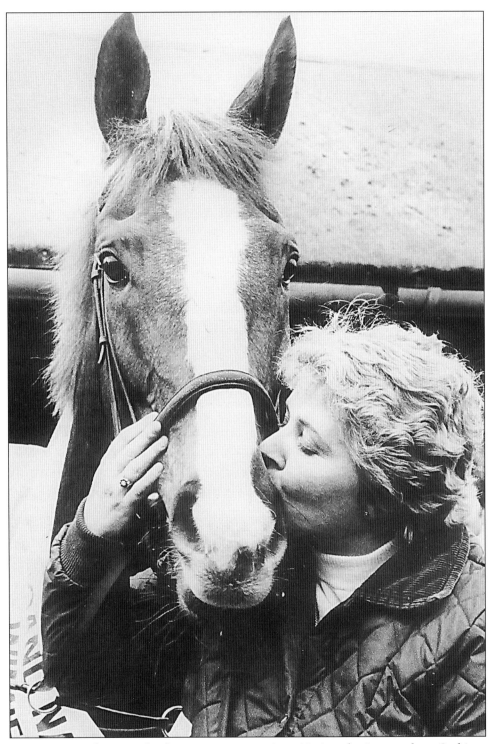

Jenny Pitman became the first woman to train a National winner when Corbiere triumphed in 1983.

trained by Nicky Henderson and had missed the previous season through injury. Although he had only returned from the lengthy lay-off four weeks before, Spartan Missile had since won a race at Newbury and his popularity and previous Aintree achievements saw him start at 9/1. Having broken a bone in a knee earlier in his career, Mid Day Gun had been brought back to prime form under trainer John Webber and was not without a chance, having won two of his last five races. For jockey Graham McCourt, Mid Day Gun would be a first ride in the Grand National. Although his form during the season had been poor, Beacon Time could boast a winning effort over the mighty fences, having claimed the Topham Trophy in 1982, and was the latest attempt by Jonjo O'Neill to cure the Aintree frustration that had dogged him for too long, while former Irish Grand National winner King Spruce gave Mrs Joy Carrier a realistic chance of becoming the first victorious female rider in the race.

With, as always, a fever of expectation before the start of the Grand National, the tape rose and the forty-one runners, led by the now-customary bold charge from Delmoss, headed for the first of thirty fences. Joined by the white face of Corbiere at the opening flight, Delmoss took off in front, but for the well-backed Mid Day Gun and outsiders Tower Moss and Midday Welcome, the race was over almost before it had begun, as the trio crashed out immediately.

As Keengaddy and Beacon Time joined the leaders, a pair of long-shots in That's It and Mender fell out of contention at the third and fourth fences, and while their jockeys dragged themselves off the ground, Becher's Brook lay in wait for the large number still standing.

Just as in 1982, the veteran Royal Mail succumbed to the daunting fence, and he was not the only one, as King Spruce fell after being badly hampered, while Beech King and Three To One also found the feared obstacle beyond them.

Keengaddy now took them along, but the horse was carried wide at the Canal Turn and lost valuable ground, while, tragically, the ten-year-old Duncreggan suffered a fatal fall when positioned further back in the field.

Having lost some momentum at the Canal Turn, Keengaddy was soon out of the race altogether as Steve Smith-Eccles' mount took a tumble at Valentine's Brook, but Delmoss was still travelling strongly up front and the pacesetter was joined by 60/1 outsider Hallo Dandy, ridden by Welshman Neale Doughty.

The next fence to reap havoc with the field was the towering Chair. As Delmoss, Hallo Dandy, Corbiere, Grittar and Greasepaint jumped the notorious fifteenth at the head of affairs, the number of contestants behind them was significantly reduced. Pilot Officer's fall brought down outsider Williamson, while 300/1 shot Sydney Quinn unfortunately landed in the trench before the fence. With Canford Ginger and O'er The Border both departing and Arrigle Boy shooting his jockey over the fence having refused, the famous fence had claimed its fair share of victims yet again.

As the second circuit began, the race started to warm up considerably. Delmoss, now in the veteran stage of his career, could not keep up the pace, and it was Hallo Dandy who took up the running at the eighteenth, with Corbiere, Colonel Christy,

Hallo Dandy (24), Colonel Christy (centre) and Corbiere fly a fence during the second circuit.

Greasepaint, Grittar and Yer Man still very much in contention. But behind the leaders, the rest of the field was cutting up drastically as Carrow Boy and Menford departed at the big ditch, while Bonum Omen's challenge was lost among the jungle of loose horses as the nine-year-old eventually refused.

Approaching Becher's for the second time it was Hallo Dandy on the outside who held a fractional lead over Corbiere, who stuck to the inside path. Between the two was Colonel Christy, who was running a superb race for a 66/1 chance, and then came Greasepaint and Grittar. All the leaders negotiated the fence safely but, out of contention at the time, Hywel Davies was unseated from Spartan Missile after the horse went down on his knees on landing.

Over the Canal Turn and Valentine's, Hallo Dandy and Corbiere began to turn on the pressure with a series of breathtaking leaps, and with both Colonel Christy and Grittar tiring as the race progressed, it was left to Greasepaint and the lightly-weighted Yer Man to throw down a challenge to the leading duo. Two fences from home, the battle was on in earnest, with Corbiere still going bravely in front, but

Hallo Dandy's bid was starting to wither on the soft ground. At this stage, none were going better than Mr Colin Magnier on the Irish threat Greasepaint, as Yer Man's gallant run also now hit the wall.

Corbiere and jockey Ben De Haan surged clear as they magnificently cleared the last and the partnership had shaken off all but Greasepaint as they reached the elbow. Three lengths down entering the closing stages, Greasepaint began to dramatically reel in Corbiere as the roar from the crowd turned in to a thunderous crescendo. Just as it looked like the Irish horse was going to prevail, the winning post arrived and Corbiere had again displayed tremendous courage and battling qualities to deny the runner-up by three-quarters of a length. Yer Man and Hallo Dandy, further back, had both run well above expectations in claiming the minor places, with Grittar putting in another cracking effort to take fifth position.

The day belonged to Jenny Pitman, who became the first woman to train the Grand National winner through the ultra-tough Corbiere, and it was with a high degree of emotion that she greeted her cherished chestnut in splendid winning enclosure scenes that fully demonstrated the true meaning of triumph in such a prestigious race.

Mrs Pitman had held a training licence since 1975 and Corbiere had been with her from the age of three. The horse had spent most of the previous season on the sidelines with injury, and it was a convincing tribute to his trainer's abilities that Corbiere had achieved all that he had.

Corbiere was the youngest winner, at eight, since Red Rum first won in 1973, and another with youth on his side was the winning jockey, Ben De Haan, who was just twenty-three, as was the victorious owner, Mr Bryan Burrough.

Once again, a romantic and heart-warming story had been suitably scripted, as only the Grand National can do, and as the dust settled on the groundbreaking 1983 contest, all that remained now was for the future of the race to be decided once and for all.

HORSE/FATE	AGE/WEIGHT	JOCKEY	ODDS
1st **CORBIERE**	8.11-4	B. DE HAAN	13/1
2nd **GREASEPAINT**	8.10-7	MR C. MAGNIER	14/1
3rd **YER MAN**	8.10-0	T.V. O'CONNELL	80/1
4th **HALLO DANDY**	9.10-1	N. DOUGHTY	60/1
5th Grittar	10.11-12	P. Barton	6/1*
6th Peaty Sandy	9.11-3	T.G. Dun	12/1
7th Political Pop	9.11-3	G. Bradley	28/1
8th Venture To Cognac	10.11-12	Mr O. Sherwood	28/1
9th Colonel Christy	8.10-0	P. Hobbs	66/1
10th Delmoss	13.10-3	W. Smith	50/1
Tacroy - *Pulled Up*	9.11-9	F. Berry	33/1
Spartan Missile - *Unseated Rider*	11.11-7	H. Davies	9/1
King Spruce - *Fell*	9.11-4	Mrs J. Carrier	28/1
Royal Mail - *Fell*	13.11-4	Mr T. Thomson Jones	50/1
The Lady's Master - *Ran Out*	12.11-2	Mr W.P. Mullins	200/1
Carrow Boy - *Fell*	11.10-12	G. Newman	33/1
Bonum Omen - *Refused*	9.10-9	K. Mooney	15/2
Mid Day Gun - *Fell*	9.10-8	G. McCourt	14/1
Pilot Officer - *Fell*	8.10-7	S. Morshead	22/1
Beacon Time - *Pulled Up*	9.10-6	J.J. O'Neill	25/1
Beech King - *Fell*	9.10-8	Mr P. Duggan	60/1
Fortina's Express - *Pulled Up*	9.10-3	P. Scudamore	20/1
Hot Tomato - *Fell*	11.10-2	J. Burke	100/1
Three To One - *Fell*	12.10-2	P. Tuck	25/1
Duncreggan - *Fell*	10.10-0	G. McGlinchley	75/1
Keengaddy - *Fell*	10.10-0	S. Smith-Eccles	15/1
Mender - *Fell*	12.10-1	A. Webber	50/1
Menford - *Refused*	8.10-0	M. Perrett	100/1
Oakprime - *Pulled Up*	8.10-5	R. Linley	66/1
The Vintner - *Refused*	12.10-0	C. Grant	66/1
Arrigle Boy - *Refused*	11.10-1	C. Pimlott	100/1
Artistic Prince - *Refused*	12.10-0	C. Brown	66/1
O'er The Border - *Refused*	9.10-12	Mr P. O'Connor	200/1
Canford Ginger - *Pulled Up*	8.10-0	J.H. Davies	33/1
Monty Python - *Refused*	11.10-2	P. O'Brien	150/1
Williamson - *Brought Down*	9.10-0	C. Mann	100/1
Midday Welcome - *Fell*	12.10-0	Mrs G. Rees	500/1
Sydney Quinn - *Fell*	11.10-0	P. Double	300/1
That's It - *Fell*	9.10-0	G. Holmes	200/1
Tower Moss - *Fell*	10.10-1	R. Rowe	300/1
Never Tamper - *Refused*	8.10-0	J. Williams	500/1

1984
HALLO DANDY

It was a brand new Grand National flavour that arrived in time for the 1984 race. Whisky giants Seagram, led by Major Ivan Straker, stepped in and agreed to sponsor the race for the next five years, with an option for five more. Outgoing chief Bill Davies, enabling the Grand National to be controlled totally by the Jockey Club, accepted an eventual sum of £3.4 million for the racecourse. New rules were also introduced, with the safety limit for runners being set at forty, while the revamped entry requirements made a greater number of horses eligible for the race. With plans to rebuild the grandstand and with the richest prize in Grand National history on offer to the winner, the great race's new hierarchy had at last provided the solid future the event so richly deserved.

As if to celebrate the newfound security of the famous race, and no doubt influenced by the considerable changes that had been made, a massive entry of 141 horses was originally submitted for the contest. With the going on the day itself riding good, a maximum field turned out for the first race in the 'new era' of Aintree.

Back again and looking for a repeat victory was last season's hero Corbiere. Jenny Pitman had not been at all happy with race handicapper, Captain Christopher Mordaunt, for designating her chestnut a colossal twelve stone to carry, and had subsequently dismissed the chances of her horse winning while shouldering such a big weight. To make matters worse, Corbiere's season had been interrupted by injury, and although Mrs Pitman had recently landed the Cheltenham Gold Cup with Burrough Hill Lad, Corbiere clearly arrived at Aintree with form inferior to the previous year.

The betting public also realised the odds were stacked against Corbiere achieving the double, and instead turned to the horse he had bravely beaten last year, Greasepaint. Having changed owners from last season, Greasepaint also had a new trainer in Dermot Weld, and the Irish raider's new handler reported the horse in grand shape for his second assault on the National. Having come nicely in to form with a pleasing second at Navan in March, Greasepaint topped the market at 9/1.

Having run a marvellous race on soft ground the previous season, Hallo Dandy had been given a light campaign on route to another tilt at the National. With an early season victory at Ayr behind him, the horse received a mid-season break from trainer Gordon Richards. After a promising reappearance at the Scottish track three weeks prior to the big race, the trainer declared himself even more confident about Hallo Dandy's chances than he had been before Lucius won in 1978.

Experienced Aintree campaigners Grittar and Spartan Missile both returned for another attempt at the race, but undoubtedly had a lot of weight to carry, and it was a host of newcomers that supplied numerous alternative betting options for racegoers and punters.

Among those to command interest were Lucky Vane, Broomy Bank, Eliogarty, Midnight Love and Two Swallows. Lucky Vane had enjoyed a hugely successful season with three victories, including the marathon Eider Chase at Newcastle where his stamina was put on display. With a Grand National-winning trainer in Toby Balding and a winning jockey in John Burke, Lucky Vane held second place in the market on 12/1, alongside Grittar and Broomy Bank. The latter, trained by John Edwards, had risen to prominence with a win in the Kim Muir Chase at the Cheltenham Festival after a long lay-off due to injury, while the Irish hunter-chaser Eliogarty, was a previous winner of Cheltenham's Foxhunter Chase, and sparked a substantial ante-post gamble after winning his only race of the season at Wexford. Jockey Chris Grant's partner Midnight Love had recorded a string of victories during the season, including most recently a win at Haydock Park, while the bold jumping grey Two Swallows had roared in to form with a recent triumph at Nottingham.

With an extremely competitive field gathered at the start, the Aintree crowd settled down to enjoy the first Grand National under the Seagram banner, and it was the David Nicholson-trained Burnt Oak who set an explosive gallop to the first fence.

With Peter Scudamore's mount continuing to blaze a trail up front, it was surprising that no horses fell at the first two fences. Golden Trix did, however, come down at the big ditch, but the rest of the field remained intact as they squared up to the considerable challenge of Becher's Brook.

Striding along at a terrific pace, Burnt Oak was at least ten lengths clear at the famous obstacle and took the fence well. Behind him, however, the casualties were starting to arrive as Midnight Love, Hazy Dawn, Three To One and Clonthturtin all crashed out of the action.

The only female rider in the race, Miss Valerie Alder, was a faller from 33/1 shot Bush Guide at the Canal turn, and out in the country, Burnt Oak continued to dictate proceedings from Greasepaint, Imperial Black, Corbiere and Tacroy. The leader plunged through the twelfth fence, but survived and led the field back on to the racecourse.

At the mighty Chair fence, Ashley House and Carl's Wager, the Michael Dickinson-trained pair, both came to grief, but thirty-one of the runners were still on their feet as Burnt Oak, though not so far in front by now, journeyed out for the second circuit followed by a glory-hungry pack featuring Greasepaint, Earthstopper, Grittar, Two Swallows, Tacroy, Spartan Missile and Corbiere.

After such a bold display of front-running, it was inevitable that Burnt Oak would tire, and by the eighteenth he had begun to fade, with Earthstopper and Greasepaint eager to take over. Two that had made very steady progress through the field were Eliogarty and Hallo Dandy, and the pair were rapidly making ground on the leaders.

At Becher's for a second time, the crowds looked on in awe as Eliogarty moved up on the outside to dispute the lead with Greasepaint and Two Swallows, while Earthstopper put in a breath-taking leap towards the inner. Hallo Dandy jumped right into contention as well as the race began to heat up.

Eliogarty made an atrocious mistake at Valentine's which seemed to knock the stuffing out of him, and it was now old adversaries Greasepaint and Hallo Dandy who began a procession over the next line of fences, and crossing the Melling Road, the pair

Irish chaser Greasepaint, runner-up to Corbiere in 1983, has to settle for second again as he trails the eventual winners, Hallo Dandy and Welsh jockey Neale Doughty.

had developed a clear lead over Earthstopper, with Two Swallows, Lucky Vane and Corbiere struggling to catch them.

The leading duo had drawn further away by the second last and Hallo Dandy, relishing the better ground, put in a fine jump to lead Greasepaint in to the final fence. Again, Hallo Dandy delivered a bold leap and quickly opened up an advantage over the Irish horse on the flat.

Just as it looked as though Hallo Dandy would gain an unsurpassable lead, the horse began to wander off a racing line and swayed over to the stand side. Cheered on by hoards of favourite-backers, Greasepaint summoned up a courageous final run to charge at Hallo Dandy, just as he had done when battling Corbiere the year before. But although the two were on opposite sides of the straight, giving the appearance of an extremely close finish, Hallo Dandy had found an extra burst of power and, with significantly less weight on his back than his rival, powered home by four lengths.

The gallant Greasepaint had given everything once more to finish second. Corbiere had run a superb race, considering the hefty burden placed upon him, and had eaten up the ground at the finish to come home third, ahead of Lucky Vane. The one sad note of an enthralling race was the death of the brave Earthstopper. After running a tremendous race, where he had been in contention for a long way, the ten-year-old collapsed and died after finishing a worthy fifth of the record twenty-three horses that completed the course.

For Hallo Dandy, the promise he had shown on his Grand National debut had gloriously been fulfilled this time around under the brilliant guidance of jockey Neale Doughty. The blistering early pace had initially caught out Hallo Dandy and he was forced to bide his time towards the back of the field for a while. But with expert horsemanship, Doughty brought his mount through to challenge by the second Becher's, and although Greasepaint posed a serious threat to the Welshman's glory bid two from home, Hallo Dandy displayed resources of stamina and finishing speed to win the day.

Hallo Dandy was owned by insurance broker Mr Richard Shaw, and he had purchased the horse, formerly trained by Donald McCain, shortly before the 1983 National.

For Gordon Richards, it was another example of his masterful training skills, and he now had a second National winner to take proudly back to his Cumbria stables, following Lucius' win in 1978.

Hallo Dandy had handsomely rewarded Richards for the confidence his trainer had shown in him, and as another epic Grand National adventure came to a close, those who truly loved the event could look forward to next year's contest and beyond with a heart-warming feeling of security, safe in the knowledge the great race was here to stay.

HORSE/FATE	AGE/WEIGHT	JOCKEY	ODDS
1st **HALLO DANDY**	10.10-2	N. DOUGHTY	13/1
2nd **GREASEPAINT**	9.11-2	T. CARMODY	9/1*
3rd **CORBIERE**	9.12-0	B. DE HAAN	16/1
4th **LUCKY VANE**	9.10-13	J. BURKE	12/1
5th Earthstopper	10.11-1	R. Rowe	33/1
6th Two Swallows	11.10-0	A. Webber	28/1
7th Fethard Friend	9.10-12	G. Newman	22/1
8th Broomy Bank	9.10-12	Mr A.J. Wilson	12/1
9th Jivago De Neuvy	9.11-0	Mr R. Grand	50/1
10th Grittar	11.11-10	J. Francome	12/1
11th Hill Of Slane	8.10-2	S. Smith-Eccles	33/1
12th Tacroy	10.10-7	F. Berry	28/1
13th Doubleuagain	10.10-5	T. Morgan	100/1
14th Beech King	10.10-1	P. Kiely	66/1
15th Eliogarty	9.11-5	Mr D. Hassett	16/1
16th Spartan Missile	12.11-4	Mr J. White	18/1
17th Yer Man	9.10-2	T.V. O'Connell	25/1
18th Fauloon	9.10-13	W. Smith	50/1
19th Another Captain	12.10-1	A. Stringer	66/1
20th Mid Day Gun	10.10-3	G. McCourt	40/1
21st Poyntz Pass	9.10-5	H. Rogers	100/1
22nd Jacko	12.10-4	S. Morshead	66/1
23rd Canford Ginger	9.10-1	C. Brown	100/1
Ashley House - *Fell*	10.11-13	G. Bradley	20/1
Midnight Love - *Fell*	9.11-4	C. Grant	28/1
Silent Valley - *Pulled Up*	11.10-8	T.G. Dun	33/1
Hazy Dawn - *Fell*	9.10-9	Mr W.P. Mullins	100/1
Burnt Oak - *Pulled Up*	8.10-7	P. Scudamore	25/1
Imperial Black - *Fell*	8.10-7	C. Hawkins	50/1
Bush Guide - *Fell*	8.10-5	Miss Valerie Alder	33/1
The Drunken Duck - *Pulled Up*	11.10-3	A. Brown	100/1
Door Step - *Fell*	8.10-2	Mr J. Queally	100/1
Pilot Officer - *Refused*	9.10-2	Mr A. Sharpe	33/1
Carl's Wager - *Fell*	9.10-2	Mr R.J. Beggan	28/1
Three To One - *Fell*	13.10-2	P. Tuck	66/1
Roman General - *Unseated Rider*	11.10-3	Major M. Wallace	100/1
Fortune Seeker - *Fell*	9.10-0	P. Barton	100/1
Golden Trix - *Fell*	9.10-1	K. Mooney	50/1
Clonthturtin - *Fell*	10.10-0	T.J. Taafe	100/1
Kumbi - *Fell*	9.10-0	K. Doolan	100/1

1985
LAST SUSPECT

The first four horses home from the previous year's race all lined up again in 1985 and each held a prominent position in a competitive and open betting market.

Of the four proven Aintree performers, Greasepaint held a share of favouritism following a season that had been geared towards the Grand National, and hopes of the horse becoming the bride instead of the bridesmaid were high. Greasepaint had pleased trainer Dermot Weld and jockey Tommy Carmody with some encouraging efforts in the build up to the big race and was, as ever, a popular selection for punters on the day. The main worry this year for the Irish chaser was that the ground was on the soft side and this was considered a stumbling block to his chances.

Joining Greasepaint as 13/2 market leader was one of the hottest chasing prospects in the land, the eight-year-old newcomer West Tip. Ridden by the rising star from Northern Ireland, Richard Dunwoody, West Tip came to Aintree having won four races in a row, including the Ritz Club Handicap Chase at the Cheltenham Festival. With the task of facing thirty fearsome fences awaiting him, the horse had already proven himself an ultra-tough customer, having survived a shuddering collision with a lorry earlier in his life that had left behind a huge scar. Extremely well weighted at 10st 1lb, West Tip clearly possessed a major chance.

Having dislocated a shoulder eight days before the National, Welshman Neale Doughty was forced to sit and watch in frustration as Hallo Dandy attempted to win the race for the second consecutive year. His place was taken by Graham Bradley, whose best effort in the race had been seventh on Political Pop in 1983. Hallo Dandy had risen 10lb in the weights since last year, and the better going he clearly loved was absent this time around. With four runs behind him in another light campaign, the horse had been a remote fifth on his latest start at Ayr, having been off the course since November 1983.

Top weight again was another Grand National specialist in the enormously popular Corbiere. Like Hallo Dandy, Corbiere was missing his regular pilot, Ben De Haan, but in Peter Scudamore, he had a more-than-capable replacement. Having been freshened up with a spell of hunting over the winter months, Corbiere had returned to winning race-course form when scoring at Chepstow on his latest run. Yet another bold showing was expected from Jenny Pitman's chestnut, and the horse started a well-backed 9/1.

Fourth and seventh respectively in the 1984 race, Lucky Vane and Fethard Friend both attracted a good deal of betting interest. Lucky Vane had run a superb trial for Aintree when winning over four miles at Cheltenham in January, beating Corbiere in the process, while Fethard Friend's recent win at Wolverhampton had him included on many 'each-way' lists at 16/1.

Other interesting candidates on this occasion were Drumlargan, Classified and Last Suspect. The Irish hope, Drumlargan, was to be John Francome's last chance of adding a Grand National to a sparkling career, while Classified had recorded three wins and two seconds in his last seven runs, but was usually recognised for running over shorter

A late change of heart from his owner, the Duchess of Westminster, allowed Last Suspect to become the hero of 1985, giving trainer Tim Forster his third winner in the race after Well To Do and Ben Nevis.

distances. Running in the colours made famous by the legendary Arkle, the inconsistent Last Suspect was the representative of Anne, Duchess of Westminster and two-time winning trainer Tim Forster. The horse's hopes appeared slim, however, having been disappointingly pulled up on his latest start.

The dark horse for the 1985 race was the Yorkshire-based Mr Snugfit. Handed a featherweight of ten stone, the strapping eight-year-old had rocketed his way in to recognition by capturing five races during the season, including a three-and-a-half mile event at Nottingham last time out. Trained in the north by Mick Easterby, Mr Snugfit's staying qualities presented Phil Tuck with a golden opportunity to capture a first Grand National.

On an overcast afternoon with construction work providing the backdrop, the maximum field of forty galloped away at the start of the race, with Corbiere's big white face showing prominently on the inside as they came to the first fence.

Hallo Dandy quickly brought back memories of Gay Trip and Aldaniti, as he became the third horse in recent times to fall at the first the year after winning, and he was joined unceremoniously on the ground by Talon, Solihull Sport and Bashful Lad.

Recent Cheltenham Festival winner Northern Bay bowed out at the second, while outsider Crosa demolished the big ditch, where Knockawad and Shady Deal were also casualties.

The 50/1 shot Dudie, a risky-jumping seven-year-old, had careered into the lead at the third, and on the run down to Becher's Brook, it was he that called the shots from Corbiere, Roman Bistro and New Zealand-rider Mr Denis Gray on Glenfox. With the fence looking as beastly as ever, Dudie landed in front, but behind him, Tacroy and Hill Of Slane were put out of the race.

Despite making a hash of Valentine's Brook, Dudie had built a tidy lead over the chasing pack, headed by Glenfox, Corbiere, Roman Bistro, Classified, Imperial Black, Greasepaint and Musso, but Lucky Vane's race had ended prematurely as the horse unfortunately broke down going to the tenth.

By the time they headed back on to the racecourse, Dudie had made a series of errors and had been jumping awkwardly, yet at the Chair, he was foot perfect and still going strongly. Joint favourite Greasepaint made an awful mistake at the monster obstacle, which knocked him back a number of places. Conversely, West Tip joined the leaders for the first time with a brilliant and fluent jump.

The second circuit began with the erratic Dudie ploughing over to the far side of the track, losing valuable ground as he did so, and over the next line of fences, an established order emerged. Corbiere, still going down the inside, was jumping like a buck, with West Tip and the Robert Stronge-ridden Rupertino also vying for the lead towards the centre. These were followed by Greasepaint, Scot Lane, Last Suspect and Broomy Bank and, with Dudie putting in one bad jump too many and departing at the nineteenth, the field sailed down to Becher's again.

With Dunwoody enjoying a tremendous first ride in the race, the leading trio arrived at the devilish Brook with West Tip travelling smoothly. But the whole picture of the race changed as West Tip, untidy on his take-off, crumbled to the ground on the landing side and was then knocked by a loose horse. Scudamore now sensed victory on Corbiere and he launched his mount into every fence that followed. The horse responded magnificently, soaring the unique obstacles in fine fashion. His nearest challengers were Rupertino, Last Suspect and Greasepaint, and the quartet had gained a handy advantage over Classified and the improving Mr Snugfit, jumping down the back straight.

Having been well down the field at the halfway stage, Phil Tuck had been quietly edging Mr Snugfit closer to the leaders as the race developed and, all of a sudden, the partnership were right in contention rounding the turn for home. With Rupertino's challenge fading, Last Suspect having made mistakes and Greasepaint under pressure at the second last, the race now appeared to lie between Corbiere and Mr Snugfit.

With a monumental difference in weight separating the pair, Mr Snugfit sailed past the former winner with a bold leap two out and blatantly had only to jump the last fence to win, and although the northern challenger did so slightly slowly, he was soon clear on the flat.

Corbiere was going backwards and Greasepaint could offer no more, while Last Suspect was only fourth jumping the last. Yet it was at the elbow that Mr Snugfit first looked like losing the race. Having to be cajoled by Phil Tuck, he was clearly slowing down and, almost unbelievably, Last Suspect was putting in a flying finish on the outside.

Encouraged frantically by jockey Hywel Davies, Last Suspect got up in the shadow of the post to pip Mr Snugfit in the most thrilling of conclusions. The winner had produced an awesome late burst, having seemed a beaten horse just moments before, to deliver heartbreak in the final strides to Phil Tuck and Mr Snugfit. Once more, Aintree-lovers Corbiere and Greasepaint had run marvellous races, especially the former, to take third and fourth, while eleven horses completed the gruelling test in total.

Of the beaten horses, West Tip was clearly running a fantastic race when coming to grief, and ironically, Dunwoody was actually attached to the winning Tim Forster stable.

The colours once carried to distinction by Arkle had now triumphed in the biggest race of all, but if it had not been for the enthusiastic persuasion of jockey Davies, the outcome might have been very different. Neither Anne, Duchess of Westminster or Tim Forster had wanted to run Last Suspect after the horse's most recent performance, in which he had shown no sparkle when pulling up. It was only Davies' telephone conversation with the owner that prevented Last Suspect from being withdrawn and the win culminated a remarkable turnaround for a jockey who had almost been killed in a fall at Doncaster the year before.

Although the victory came as a surprise, Forster had now trained a trio of Grand National winners, while the Duchess had previously owned the 1967 winner Foinavon, although that one had slipped through her grasp by the time of his famous victory. Last Suspect though, was very much hers, and it was with a gracious and immediate decision that the owner elected to retire her sometime temperamental, but on this occasion extremely game, Grand National hero.

HORSE/FATE	AGE/WEIGHT	JOCKEY	ODDS
1st **LAST SUSPECT**	**11.10-5**	**H. DAVIES**	**50/1**
2nd **MR SNUGFIT**	**8.10-0**	**P. TUCK**	**12/1**
3rd **CORBIERE**	**10.11-10**	**P. SCUDAMORE**	**9/1**
4th **GREASEPAINT**	**10.10-13**	**T. CARMODY**	**13/2***
5th Classified	9.10-7	J. White	20/1
6th Imperial Black	9.10-1	C. Hawkins	66/1
7th Rupertino	10.10-0	R. Stronge	33/1
8th Scot Lane	12.10-1	C. Smith	28/1
9th Glenfox	8.10-0	Mr D. Gray	50/1
10th Blackrath Prince	9.10-0	B. Reilly	66/1
11th Captain Parkhill	12.10-0	C. Grant	100/1
Drumlargan - *Pulled Up*	11.11-8	J. Francome	8/1
Lucky Vane - *Pulled Up*	10.10-13	J. Burke	10/1
Hallo Dandy - *Fell*	11.10-12	G. Bradley	14/1
Broomy Bank - *Refused*	10.10-7	Mr A.J. Wilson	33/1
Fethard Friend - *Pulled Up*	10.10-7	P. Barton	16/1
Tacroy - *Fell*	11.10-3	A. Stringer	33/1
West Tip - *Fell*	8.10-1	R. Dunwoody	13/2*
Kumbi - *Fell*	10.10-0	K. Doolan	25/1
Musso - *Pulled Up*	9.10-0	Mr S. Sherwood	50/1
Dudie - *Fell*	7.10-0	A. Mullins	50/1
Shady Deal - *Fell*	12.10-3	R. Rowe	50/1
Tubbertelly - *Refused*	8.10-1	T.J. Taafe	50/1
Talon - *Fell*	10.10-0	A. Webber	33/1
Onapromise - *Pulled Up*	9.10-5	A. Brown	100/1
Knockawad - *Fell*	8.10-0	K.F. O'Brien	66/1
Hill Of Slane - *Fell*	9.10-2	S. Smith-Eccles	25/1
Royal Appointment - *Fell*	10.10-0	P. Gill	66/1
Solihull Sport - *Fell*	11.10-0	S. Morshead	100/1
Clonthturtin - *Pulled Up*	11.10-5	Mr T. Th'n Jones	50/1
Fauloon - *Fell*	10.10-2	K. Mooney	66/1
Bashful Lad - *Fell*	10.10-3	G. McCourt	50/1
Crosa - *Fell*	10.10-0	S. Moore	100/1
Never Tamper - *Pulled Up*	10.10-3	C. Brown	200/1
Roman Bistro - *Refused*	9.10-3	P. Nicholls	150/1
Leney Dual - *Fell*	10.10-8	Mr D. Pitcher	100/1
Our Cloud - *Refused*	9.10-0	Mr J. Queally	150/1
Immigrate - *Fell*	12.10-0	J. Hansen	100/1
Greenhill Hall - *Pulled Up*	9.10-0	D. Wilkinson	200/1
Northern Bay - *Fell*	9.10-1	P. Hobbs	66/1

1986
WEST TIP

Despite Anne Duchess of Westminster's pledge to retire Last Suspect following the horse's exciting win the year before, the twelve-year-old went back in training for another season with Captain Tim Forster, and the change of heart yielded two wins from two starts and a place in the 1986 Grand National line up.

With Last Suspect back in the fold, it meant the three most recent winners of the race would all be running, as both Corbiere and Hallo Dandy were back again.

But it was the two horses that caught the eye most in defeat the previous season that headed the betting market this time, Mr Snugfit and West Tip. Having been purchased by Mr Terry Ramsden, Mr Snugfit was again to be ridden by Phil Tuck. The horse had been specifically trained for the Grand National throughout the season by Mick Easterby and had performed admirably on his latest start under a big weight, and stable confidence in the northern raider was strong. This optimism was shared by the betting public, who made the horse the warm 13/2 favourite.

His dramatic exit at Becher's Brook the previous year had done little to deter West Tip's spirit and a recent win over Beau Ranger at Newbury had been significantly franked when that same horse had overturned the high-class Wayward Lad just two days before the National. Richard Dunwoody, at twenty-two, was the youngest rider competing in the 1986 race, and hopes were high that the jockey could guide Michael Oliver's charge round for a big run.

The horses that already had Grand National experience dominated the market, but one newcomer who found himself among the leading fancies was the eight-year-old Door Latch. Owned by ninety-one-year-old Mr Jim Joel, Door Latch had a cluster of solid form behind him. The horse had won at Ascot during the season while also registering bold displays in both the Hennessy Gold Cup and Peter Marsh Chase. His jockey Richard Rowe knew his way round the course, having finished fifth on Earthstopper in 1984, and Door Latch was a popular selection on the day at 9/1 to land a first Grand National for the famous black and scarlet colours of his owner.

With Aintree regular Greasepaint now eleven and a small race at Tramore being his only win for a long time, many considered the chance of an Irish success lay elsewhere this time, with nine-year-old Monanore a striking candidate. Three wins in his last four runs, including a recent straightforward victory at Gowran Park, had brought Tom Morgan's mount in to the National picture, and he was a live outsider at 22/1.

A couple of late purchases were secured shortly before the big race when the Cheveley Park Stud owners David and Pat Thompson acquired Classified and Northern Bay. Both horses had run in the National the previous year and Classified came in to the race as a fresh horse, having had just three runs during the season. On his latest run, he had finished sixth to stablemate The Tsarevich, also a National contender, in the Mildmay of Flete Chase at the Cheltenham Festival. Like Classified, The Tsarevich's best form was at much shorter distances than the National trip, but his recent success, together with the

Up-and-coming star Richard Dunwoody salutes West Tip's emphatic victory in 1986.

fact that Seagram chief Major Ivan Straker owned him, generated a lot of interest in the horse. His trainer, Nicky Henderson, was however, undecided as to which of The Tsarevich or Classified would put in the better display.

Other interesting runners in the 1986 Grand National were Knock Hill, Young Driver and Essex. Mark Dwyer's stamina-packed mount Knock Hill had staked his claim for Aintree consideration when winning at Cheltenham and Warwick in January and had since been freshened up for the big race, while Young Driver, an injury-plagued nine-year-old, had been especially prepared for the race in Scotland by trainer John Wilson and had only narrowly been beaten by Hallo Dandy at Ayr in March. Essex meanwhile, was representing Czechoslovakia, and was the automatic top weight, having not run three times in the country. Unusually for such a race, the horse was still an entire, and was ridden by his trainer, forty-year-old Vaclav Chaloupka.

With an inch of snow falling on the track overnight, accompanied by a day of cloud and drizzle, the ground at Aintree had been left lifeless, with the turf cutting up noticeably in places. Even so, the customary roar greeted the runners as the starter sent them on their way, and almost immediately, the diminutive Czech stallion Essex had pulled his way to the front in the middle of the track and was joined by rank outsider Doubleuagain as they met the first fence. The first shock of the race came swiftly as Door Latch slid to the ground following a clumsy take-off, and he was joined on the floor by Port Askaig.

With Lantern Lodge falling at the second, a pattern had quickly emerged up front with Tacroy and Douleuagain bowling along in the lead, together with the free-running Essex. Another recognised front-runner, Dudie, unseated his young jockey Kevin Doolan at the big ditch, though he soon remounted, albeit some distance behind the bulk of the field.

After Door Latch's surprise exit, an even bigger gasp of shock was reserved for Aintree veteran Corbiere, as he crashed through the top of the fourth fence and fell to the ground in spectacular and unexpected fashion.

The same leaders were still in place approaching Becher's, and the white face of The Tsarevich had emerged just behind them together with Kilkilowen, while Greasepaint and West Tip were moving smoothly into position further back. With all the leaders clearing the mighty fence in grand style, Dudie, well out of contention at the back, fell and this time was out of the race for good.

Jumping Valentine's Brook and beyond, the leaders managed to stay out of trouble, but in behind them, the field was shedding some of its number. The tenth fence in particular proved troublesome as Ten Cherries plummeted to the turf when on the heels of the pacesetters, while Another Duke also went and Acarine collided with a fellow runner and was brought down.

But those that were still on their feet – and there were plenty at this stage – were now merging in to one big bunch as they came back on to the racecourse, still led by Tacroy and Doubleuagain. In the middle of the pack, the fancied Knock Hill did his best to unseat Mark Dwyer at the thirteenth, and even though the partnership survived, their chances had been badly dented, while as they took the Chair, Classified began to make eye-catching progress.

The long run to begin the second circuit saw Hallo Dandy well towards the rear of the field and clearly struggling on the unsuitable going, while even further back, Last Suspect now had no chance of repeating his heroics of the year before.

Doubleuagain's reward for a bold display was to be knocked to the ground by a loose horse while still disputing the lead at the seventeenth. Tacroy too began to tire at this point and, two fences later, a sloppy jump ended his contention.

The major players were now starting to emerge and clearing Becher's without trouble, the leading group of Kilkilowen, Classified, Northern Bay, The Tsarevich, West Tip, Young Driver, Sommelier and the rapidly improving Monanore, began to assert themselves and the group pulled clear of the rest jumping the fences out in the country.

An exciting finish looked on the cards as the contestants rounding the turn for home, as Scotland's Young Driver surged to the front past the tiring Kilkilowen, Monanore and Northern Bay, and it was he that led at the second last with Classified, Sommelier and The Tsarevich still there and Dunwoody stalking them on West Tip.

With a rousing conclusion in prospect, Chris Grant urged Young Driver clear as they jumped the final flight and most of the others were soon struggling. Not so West Tip, however, and with extreme patience and perfect timing, Dunwoody coolly waited until the elbow before unleashing his mount past the helpless Young Driver, and the second favourite galloped strongly to the line to hold the outsider comfortably by two lengths.

Richard Dunwoody punched the air in triumph as West Tip crossed the line, and there was no doubt that the best horse had won the day as he was always travelling and jumping extremely well. Young Driver was brave to the end in defeat and with his history of injuries, the achievement of trainer John Wilson to have him prepared for such a big run was admirable. Classified's chance had obviously been affected by the stamina-sapping ground, and despite running another excellent race, he did not quite see out the distance, while Mr Snugfit, who had never threatened the leaders, came from a long way back to finish fourth.

The gallant and tough West Tip had made up for the previous year's disappointment in especially convincing style and provided his trainer Michael Oliver with the victory he had promised to achieve for a long time. When Oliver was only six, he had vowed to one day win the National after ESB, who his father Roland had owned, took the 1956 race. Now his statement had come true with a horse owned by Mr Peter Luff.

As for Richard Dunwoody, excused from the ride on first-fence faller Port Askaig for retainer Tim Forster, the Grand National victory on West Tip was merely a stepping stone for the challenge he now set himself – that of becoming champion jump jockey. For the highly-talented young rider, it would be another ambition he would one day gloriously achieve.

HORSE/FATE	AGE/WEIGHT	JOCKEY	ODDS
1st **WEST TIP**	9.10-11	R. DUNWOODY	15/2
2nd **YOUNG DRIVER**	9.10-0	C. GRANT	66/1
3rd **CLASSIFIED**	10.10-3	S. SMITH-ECCLES	22/1
4th **MR SNUGFIT**	9.10-7	P. TUCK	13/2*
5th Sommelier	8.10-0	T.J. Taafe	50/1
6th Broomy Bank	11.10-3	P. Scudamore	20/1
7th The Tsarevich	10.10-7	J. White	16/1
8th Monanore	9.10-0	T. Morgan	22/1
9th Little Polveir	9.10-3	C. Brown	66/1
10th Greasepaint	11.10-9	T. Carmody	16/1
11th Northern Bay	10.10-0	P. Hobbs	33/1
12th Hallo Dandy	12.10-8	N. Doughty	16/1
13th Kilkilowen	10.11-3	K. Morgan	25/1
14th Imperial Black	10.10-0	R. Crank	66/1
15th Rupertino	11.10-0	G. Charles-Jones	66/1
16th Why Forget	10.10-7	R. Lamb	35/1
17th Gayle Warning	12.10-9	Mr A. Dudgeon	50/1
Essex - *Pulled Up*	8.12-0	Mr V. Chaloupka	100/1
Corbiere - *Fell*	11.11-7	B. De Haan	14/1
Drumlargan - *Fell*	12.11-6	T.J. Ryan	40/1
Last Suspect - *Pulled Up*	12.11-2	H. Davies	14/1
Door Latch - *Fell*	8.11-0	R. Rowe	9/1
Acarine - *Brought Down*	10.10-13	R. Stronge	33/1
Ballinacurra Lad - *Fell*	11.10-8	G. Bradley	22/1
Lantern Lodge - *Fell*	9.10-7	A. Mullins	100/1
Tracys Special - *Fell*	9.10-6	S.C. Knight	150/1
Another Duke - *Fell*	13.10-4	P. Nicholls	200/1
Plundering - *Fell*	9.10-1	S. Sherwood	25/1
Tacroy - *Unseated Rider*	12.10-1	A. Stringer	200/1
Dudie - *Fell*	8.10-0	K. Doolan	100/1
Knock Hill - *Pulled Up*	10.10-1	M. Dwyer	18/1
Ballymilan - *Unseated Rider*	9.10-0	C. Hawkins	50/1
Fethard Friend - *Pulled Up*	11.10-2	P. Barton	35/1
Late Night Extra - *Pulled Up*	10.10-2	Mr T. Thomson Jones	500/1
Master Tercel - *Fell*	10.10-7	D. Browne	150/1
St Alezan - *Brought Down*	9.10-2	C. Smith	150/1
Port Askaig - *Fell*	11.10-5	G. McCourt	35/1
Doubleuagain - *Brought Down*	12.10-0	C. Mann	500/1
Ten Cherries - *Fell*	11.10-0	A. Sharpe	66/1
Mount Oliver - *Fell*	8.10-0	J. Bryan	500/1

1987
MAORI VENTURE

Before the main event in 1987, the courageous 1981-winning partnership of Bob Champion and Aldaniti found themselves galloping down the famous track at Aintree in front of the packed grandstand. The duo had just completed a sponsored walk from Buckingham Palace to the Grand National course on behalf of the Bob Champion Cancer Trust Fund. Accompanied on their travels by a vast array of personalities, they had achieved another memorable goal by raising a large amount of money for the charity, and their return provoked a rapturous reception from all those present at Aintree.

The 1987 edition of the Grand National took place without Aintree stalwart Greasepaint, who was withdrawn at the four-day stage, while previous winners Hallo Dandy and Last Suspect had also participated in their final Nationals the year before. Another absentee on this occasion was the recent Cheltenham Gold Cup winner, The Thinker, who had generally been priced at 7/1 for Aintree glory, but was pulled out at the last minute after failing to shine in his final piece of preparatory work.

Back as favourite, however, was the previous year's winner, West Tip. Having been largely disappointing during the season, the horse finally sparkled when staying on strongly for fourth in the Gold Cup at Cheltenham. With his impressive success twelve months before still fresh in the minds of many National enthusiasts, West Tip started as a hot favourite at 5/1.

Extremely well weighted with just 10st 2lb was the dashing grey Dark Ivy, trained by Gordon Richards. The eleven-year-old had enjoyed a successful first year with the Greystoke trainer, having been formerly trained in Ireland by Bunny Cox, and Dark Ivy came to Aintree having won his last race at Ayr to go with a fine second in the marathon Eider Chase at Newcastle. With both Richards and jockey Phil Tuck particularly bullish about their horse's chance, the betting public plunged on in the hope that Dark Ivy could become the first grey horse to win the National since Nicolaus Silver in 1961.

The Nicky Henderson-trained pair of Classified and The Tsarevich were back after impressive showings in the 1986 race. Classified was the more fancied of the two as The Tsarevich had not started serious work until after Christmas, with his only run of the season coming at the recent Cheltenham Festival.

After his uncharacteristic fall of a year ago, the now twelve-year-old Corbiere returned to Aintree for a fifth and final run in the National, but it was Jenny Pitman's second runner, the lightly-raced Smith's Man who had stronger recent form, and the talented grey horse had captured the Whitbread Trophy over the National fences at the meeting the previous year.

Although he had finished third in the season's Hennessy Gold Cup and second on his latest start in the Grand Military Gold Cup at Sandown, Maori Venture was thought to be too inconsistent and careless a jumper to get round the demanding Grand National course. Even his trainer, Andy Turnell, admitted the horse was inclined to make mistakes and considered his other runner, Tracys Special, the better option of the two prospects. As it was, Maori Venture was generally an afterthought in the betting at 28/1.

A souvenir magazine from the 1987 edition of the Grand National.

For various reasons, Plundering, The Ellier, Bewley's Hill and Valencio attracted their fair share of attention. Plundering, a faller in the previous year's Grand National, was a former winner of the Whitbread Gold Cup and had returned from a mid-season break to run well recently at Sandown, while The Ellier had risen to prominence with a win in the Kim Muir Chase at the Cheltenham Festival the month before. While those two were well fancied, Bewley's Hill and Valencio lined up as big outsiders. Bewley's Hill, from America, had won the Maryland Hunt Cup in 1984 and was ridden by his owner, Mr Dixon Stroud Jnr, while Valencio was the second consecutive National representative from Czechoslovakia, although the price of 500/1 reflected his aspirations.

With race sponsors Seagram ensuring the winning prize was the most valuable in the history of the race, the runners were called into line and were soon on their way on an extremely misty afternoon.

Having his first ever ride in the race, twenty-year-old Guy Landau sent the Stan Mellor-trained Lean Ar Aghaidh out to make the running and, approaching the first, the chestnut was right up amongst the lead with Insure, Valencio and Plundering, with Corbiere, as usual, going down the inside route. Bad mistakes saw Lucky Rew and Smartside botch their chances, and amateur rider David Pitcher, who had bought Brown Trix so he could have a ride in the race, was unseated from the horse two fences later at the big ditch.

On the rundown to Becher's Brook, Lean Ar Aghaidh had pulled into the lead in the centre of the track with Insure, Northern Bay, Classified and You're Welcome all going smoothly on his heels. Behind them though, the runners were bunching up tightly in the jostle for positions, and as the bulk of the field met the fence, the race's bleak tragedy occurred. With the Irish runner Attitude Adjuster changing directions on his approach to the fence, he unfortunately blocked the path of Dark Ivy. Badly hampered and with no room for a clean jump, the classy grey horse catapulted into the fence and ghosted to the ground, breaking his neck in a cruel and disheartening fatal fall. Bewley's Hill was brought down in the process, and as the mist thickened, the field raced on, leaving behind a sombre mood for those who had witnessed poor Dark Ivy's demise.

Travelling strongly down the inside was 200/1 shot Big Brown Bear, and at the Canal Turn he jumped through to start a running battle for the lead with Lean Ar Aghaidh that would continue throughout the race.

With most of the runners still very much in contention, it was an impressive and well-packed group that proceeded back on to the racecourse. Big Brown Bear was running a fantastic race on the inside and he was accompanied by Lean Ar Aghaidh and Northern Bay as they came to the Chair, with Miss Jacqui Oliver moving up on the outside on Eamon's Owen to make a line of four. Eamon's Owen lunged at the gaping ditch and landed hard on the other side of the fence, sending his female rider sprawling over his neck and onto the ground. Further back, Little Polveir clipped the fence and also unseated his rider, but the remainder of the field streamed over and a large number of horses shot past the teaming grandstand to enthusiastic vocal encouragement.

Retaining his lead with a fast jump at the Water, Lean Ar Aghaidh set off for a second circuit with the bold intention of leading all the way to the finish, and the chestnut was followed in his bid for glory by Big Brown Bear, Northern Bay, You're Welcome, Insure, West Tip, Attitude Adjuster, Plundering, The Tsarevich and Classified.

On the way down to Becher's for a second time, Lean Ar Aghaidh and Big Brown Bear continued their exciting duel with a series of powerful leaps, with Attitude Adjuster joining them as they approached the obstacle. One who had made steady progress towards the outside was Maori Venture, and Steve Knight had his mount well positioned as they arrived at Becher's. Lean Ar Aghaidh made a mistake which had Guy Landau's arms shooting for the sky, but he had quickly recovered and was back in the lead, while West Tip had come through strongly on the inside to threaten Big Brown Bear's position. Northern Bay began to tire and Classified unshipped his rider Steve Smith-Eccles following a slipped saddle at the Canal Turn, but a large number were still in the hunt as the race progressed to the home turn.

The unconsidered Big Brown Bear's marvellous bid finally began to falter on the run to two out, and this had left Lean Ar Aghaidh on his own in front. Just behind him, the challengers were queuing up to steal his thunder with Attitude Adjuster, Maori Venture and You're Welcome still there, while The Tsarevich was creeping up smoothly. However, West Tip was beginning to struggle, and at the second last, his chance of recording consecutive wins had all but disappeared.

Amazingly, Lean Ar Aghaidh had found another burst of energy, and a huge roar went up as he touched down in front over the last. But failing to find any more on the flat, the long-time leader was caught and finally overthrown at the elbow by Maori Venture on the outside and The Tsarevich shooting up the inside, and these two then battled out the finish.

With the white faces of both horses matching each other in a rousing finale, it was Maori Venture that proved the stronger and produced a finishing burst to beat The

A supposedly dodgy jumper, Maori Venture (5) found his niche at Aintree to win from The Tsarevich (10).

Tsarevich by five lengths, with the gutsy Lean Ar Aghaidh back in third. Although he could not stay with the leaders over the final fences, West Tip's determination saw him snatch fourth place, with You're Welcome carrying the Aldaniti colours in to fifth. Further back, The Ellier, who had been an enormous distance behind the leaders in the early stages, came home with a flourish in seventh to leave his backers frustrated and bewildered at the way he was ridden, while Corbiere completed his last National safely in twelfth, one place ahead of the game and surprising Big Brown Bear.

The twenty-two that finished were the most in history with the exception of 1984, and Maori Venture had finally given his owner Mr Jim Joel a victory in the Grand National after numerous attempts spanning many years. The often risky jumper had made up in dramatic style for his owner's disappointment the year before with Door Latch, and although Mr Joel was on a plane returning from South Africa when being informed of the horse's win, he soon decided to retire his Aintree hero and, as a fitting gesture, announced that he was leaving Maori Venture to Steve Knight in his will.

The victory was also a positive salute to Andy Turnell, who in only his second season as a trainer had prepared not only the actual winner of the Grand National, but also

Only Lean Ar Aghaidh precedes Maori Venture, with The Tsarevich close behind.

Tracys Special, who finished sixth. Maori Venture's win made up for thirteen unsuccessful rides in the race for Turnell, with his third place on Charles Dickens in 1974 being the closest he got to victory.

Controversy, as so often with the National, followed the 1987 race after the sad and much-publicised death of Dark Ivy at Becher's Brook. RSPCA members called for the fence to be altered and this left racecourse manager John Parrett to reassure all the concerned parties that suggestions to improve the race's safety would be considered. These were suggestions that were beginning to become increasingly frequent.

HORSE/FATE	AGE/WEIGHT	JOCKEY	ODDS
1st **MAORI VENTURE**	11.10-13	S.C. KNIGHT	28/1
2nd **THE TSAREVICH**	11.10-5	J. WHITE	20/1
3rd **LEAN AR AGHAIDH**	10.10-0	G. LANDAU	14/1
4th **WEST TIP**	10.11-7	R. DUNWOODY	5/1*
5th You're Welcome	11.10-2	P. Hobbs	50/1
6th Tracys Special	10.10-0	S. McNeill	50/1
7th The Ellier	11.10-0	F. Berry	18/1
8th Attitude Adjuster	7.10-6	N. Madden	25/1
9th Northern Bay	11.10-1	R. Crank	50/1
10th Monanore	10.10-3	T. Morgan	20/1
11th Smith's Man	9.10-0	M. Perrett	14/1
12th Corbiere	12.10-10	B. De Haan	12/1
13th Big Brown Bear	10.10-2	R. Stronge	200/1
14th Cranlome	9.10-0	M. Richards	500/1
15th Colonel Christy	12.10 0	S. Moore	300/1
16th Plundering	10.10-11	P. Scudamore	16/1
17th Preben Fur	10.10-0	A. Stringer	66/1
18th Bright Dream	11.10-2	R. Rowe	50/1
19th Why Forget	11.10-0	C. Grant	40/1
20th Gala Prince	10.10-0	T. Jarvis	500/1
21st Brit	8.10-1	A. Jones	500/1
22nd Insure	9.10-10	Mr C. Brooks	45/1
Bewley's Hill - *Brought Down*	10.12-0	W.B. Dixon Stroud Jnr	100/1
Valencio - *Fell*	10.12-0	R. Rowell	500/1
Drumlargan - *Pulled Up*	13.11-2	Mr G. Wragg	66/1
Classified - *Unseated Rider*	11.10-3	S. Smith-Eccles	9/1
Glenrue - *Fell*	10.10-3	B. Powell	33/1
Dark Ivy - *Fell*	11.10-2	P. Tuck	11/2
Daltmore - *Pulled Up*	9.10-0	A. Mullins	100/1
Smartside - *Fell*	12.10-0	P. Gill	100/1
Run To Me - *Pulled Up*	12.10-2	Mr N. Mitchell	150/1
Hi Harry - *Refused*	9.10-0	M. Flynn	100/1
Marcolo - *Fell*	10.10-0	P. Leech	66/1
Brown Trix - *Unseated Rider*	9.10-8	Mr D.F. Pitcher	100/1
Little Polveir - *Unseated Rider*	10.10-2	C. Brown	33/1
Eamon's Owen - *Unseated Rider*	10.10-0	Miss Jacqui Oliver	200/1
Brown Veil - *Pulled Up*	12.10-1	Mr M. Armytage	200/1
Lucky Rew - *Fell*	12.10-0	C. Mann	500/1
Le Bambino - *Pulled Up*	10.10-2	C. Warren	500/1
Spartan Orient - *Knocked Over*	11.10-0	L. Harvey	500/1

1988
RHYME 'N' REASON

Favourite for the 1988 Grand National was the eight-year-old Sacred Path, who was having his first run in the race. His team of trainer Oliver Sherwood and jockey Clive Cox were also having their initial experiences with the National in their respective roles. Having won his only start of the season over three-and-a-half miles at Warwick, Sacred Path was considered a reliable jumper and certain stayer. The horse had not been out of the first three places in his ten completed chases and was a model of consistency, and this earned him a wave of support and a place at the top of the betting market at 17/2.

Now aged eleven, West Tip was entering his fourth Grand National battle and did so shouldering top weight of 11st 7lb. Remarkably, Richard Dunwoody's mount had failed to record a single victory since his National success in 1986 but, much like the season before, a recent encouraging effort in the Cheltenham Gold Cup proved the Aintree specialist was peaking at the right time for another challenge over the famous fences. In a close market, West Tip was once more a popular selection, and started at 11/1.

Having put up such a bold display in the 1987 race, Lean Ar Aghaidh had gone on to capture the Whitbread Gold Cup with another fine exhibition of front running and was quickly installed as one of the ante-post favourites for the 1988 Grand National. But, having had just one run during the season and with a stone more to carry at Aintree on this occasion, the bad news for Lean Ar Aghaidh was that the ground was turning against him, with a deluge of heavy rain two days before the race. The lack of fast going saw him lose his place at the head of the market to Sacred Path, and he was now listed as joint second favourite in the betting at 10/1.

Accompanying him on that mark was an interesting Aintree newcomer: the David Elsworth-trained Rhyme 'N' Reason. The nine-year-old had delivered a topsy-turvy career, which had looked full of promise when he took the Irish Grand National in 1985 as a six-year-old. Having suffered a serious dip in form in the next two seasons and haunted by jumping problems, he was transferred to Elsworth from the stable of David Murray-Smith. The horse then won four races during the build-up to the National for his new trainer as he rocketed back to form, but his old problem had resurfaced on his latest run with a fall in the Cheltenham Gold Cup. Still, he was considered a major contender by both his trainer and the betting public and rightfully took his place among the market leaders.

Two of the leading candidates from Ireland on this occasion were Hard Case and Lastofthebrownies. The well-backed Hard Case had not run over a distance further than two-and-a-half miles for two seasons but had, in Jim Dreaper, a trainer who finished second as a jockey in the 1971 race on Black Secret. Lastofthebrownies was trained by Mouse Morris and had recorded a hat-trick of wins during the season. His jockey on this occasion was Tommy Carmody, the regular partner of former Aintree specialist Greasepaint.

Durham Edition, Border Burg, The Tsarevich and Bucko all provided the 1988 race with a depth of enticing options. Trained by Arthur Stephenson, the strapping Durham Edition had won easily at Market Rasen on his latest start, having previously run well to take third place in the Hennessy Gold Cup, while Border Burg had already proved himself over the giant fences with a win in the previous year's Foxhunter's Chase. Although he had disappointed his followers during the season with a pair of below-average efforts, The Tsarevich had twice shown his liking for the Grand National's unique challenge, while Bucko, recently purchased by J.P. McManus, had run a big race in the Ritz Club Chase at the Cheltenham Festival and was looking to provide his trainer Jimmy Fitzgerald with a much-needed lift, having lost his star chaser Forgive 'N' Forget in the Cheltenham Gold Cup.

Perhaps driven by the prospect of landing the richest winning prize in Grand National history, several over-eager runners jumped off too early and snapped the starting tape. Finally, with the false start behind them, the forty-strong field began their quest, and it was the favourite, Sacred Path, that was the first to show in the middle of the track as they charged towards the first fence.

The opening obstacle had caught out many good horses through the years, and to a huge shriek of disbelief, Sacred Path agonisingly joined the list with an over-zealous jump that brought about his downfall on the landing side. Further back, outsiders Tullamarine and Hettinger also came to grief, the latter taking half the fence with him as he crashed to the floor.

After landing awkwardly over the second fence, the injury-riddled grey Smith's Man was pulled up gingerly having gone lame and, out in front, Lean Ar Aghaidh began to dispute the lead with his old rival, Big Brown Bear.

With a slipped saddle forcing Peter Hobbs to pull up You're Welcome, Gee-A and top female rider Gee Armytage joined the leaders as they ran down to Becher's Brook. As the leading group flew the mighty fence without incident, Rhyme 'N' Reason, on the wide outside, put in a bold leap but was caught out by the exaggerated drop on the landing side. Slithering and sliding onto his belly, he seemed certain to topple over, yet amazingly his jockey Brendan Powell had stayed on board, and as the horse struggled to his feet, the partnership set off in distant pursuit of the rest of the field following one of the most spectacular recoveries in Grand National history.

The leading group of Lean Ar Aghaidh, Big Brown Bear, Gee-A, Kumbi and Eton Rouge kept up the strong gallop out in the country, with Course Hunter making particular headway as the runners drew closer to the Chair. Almost unbelievably, Rhyme 'N' Reason had regained the ground he had lost at Becher's and was now in tenth position on the extreme outside, while a slow jump at the huge fence cost Big Brown Bear valuable lengths and he was never able to recapture his place.

As the second circuit got underway, the unfavourable ground was starting to take its toll on Lean Ar Aghaidh and he was clearly struggling jumping the big ditch, where the fancied Hard Case departed from the race. It was Little Polveir, running in his third National, that now had the upper hand in the middle from the ever-improving Rhyme 'N' Reason on the outside and West Tip, who was beginning to get involved on the inside, together with Course Hunter.

However, it was Peter Scudamore on Strands Of Gold that was going best of all at this stage, and heading for Becher's once more, the partnership had taken a clear lead on the

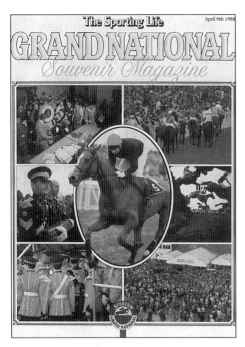 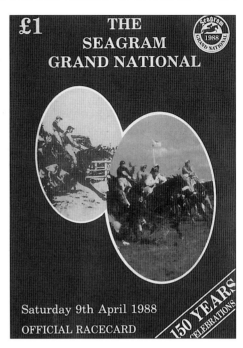

A racecard and souvenir magazine from the 1988 edition.

inside rail and attacked the fence with ferocity to try and further their advantage. However, after clouting the spruce at the top of the fence, Strands Of Gold had no chance of surviving the drop on the landing side and, to the utter frustration of Scudamore, the pair came to grief. Perhaps distracted by his rival's tumble, Course Hunter slipped down to his knees after jumping the fence, yet he too was able to make a fantastic recovery with Paul Croucher still on board, but their chances of winning had been severely dented.

A group of six had now made a break from the remainder, headed by Little Polveir, with Rhyme 'N' Reason, Durham Edition and Lastofthebrownies following him, along with Aintree veterans West Tip and Monanore, and as they jumped the fences after Valentine's Brook, it was clear that the winner would come from this group.

When Little Polveir cannoned Tom Morgan into the sky with only four fences to jump, West Tip and Rhyme 'N' Reason were left to dispute the lead, but in behind them, Durham Edition was travelling incredibly smoothly as they rounded the turn for home, and with the others under pressure, it appeared he had the race sewn up.

Jumping the final fence in superb style, the giant northern chaser strode away clear of his nearest pursuer, Rhyme 'N' Reason, and victory seemed assured. But the long run-in was to prove bitterly cruel for jockey Chris Grant for the second time in three years.

With Durham Edition unable to quicken away after the elbow, the battling Rhyme 'N' Reason wore him down and swept past Grant's mount to complete one of the most famous comebacks ever.

While Young Driver had clearly been second best to West Tip in 1986, Chris Grant had looked very much like winning this time on Durham Edition, but ultimately he had to settle for second place again. Monanore had relished the conditions and finished an honourable third with West Tip enhancing his reputation as an Aintree legend by once more coming home fourth.

With a never-say-die attitude and steely determination, the brave Rhyme 'N' Reason had triumphed in the most unlikely of circumstances. Twice he had looked a defeated horse following his early mishap at Becher's, and then when Durham Edition burst in to the lead at the last – but he had triumphed, with jockey Brendan Powell deservedly taking a large slice of the credit.

The twenty-seven-year-old Powell had suffered a completely different experience in the previous year's Grand National when breaking his arm in a fall from Glenrue, but not even a summons to the steward's office after the race to explain his apparent excessive use of the whip during the finish could conceal his euphoric joy of riding Rhyme 'N' Reason to victory.

Trainer David Elsworth was a happy man too, for not only had he trained the Grand National winner, but he had also backed him at twice his starting price! Elsworth had faced a hard time, however, to initially convince owner Miss Juliet Reed to run the horse she loved so much. In the end, all those connected with Rhyme 'N' Reason were overjoyed with his tremendous performance to capture an action-packed, highly dramatic and spectacularly exciting running of the world's greatest steeplechase.

HORSE/FATE	AGE/WEIGHT	JOCKEY	ODDS
1st RHYME 'N' REASON	9.11-0	B. POWELL	10/1
2nd DURHAM EDITION	10.10-9	C. GRANT	20/1
3rd MONANORE	11.10-4	T.J. TAAFE	33/1
4th WEST TIP	11.11-7	R. DUNWOODY	11/1
5th Attitude Adjuster	8.10-6	N. Madden	33/1
6th Friendly Henry	8.10-4	N. Doughty	100/1
7th The Tsarevich	12.10-10	J. White	18/1
8th Course Hunter	10.10-1	P. Croucher	20/1
9th Lean Ar Aghaidh	11.11-0	G. Landau	10/1
Hard Case - *Fell*	10.10-12	K. Morgan	13/1
Border Burg - *Pulled Up*	11.10-7	S. Sherwood	16/1
Little Polveir - *Unseated Rider*	11.10-7	T. Morgan	33/1
Lucisis - *Brought Down*	9.10-6	Mr J. Queally	40/1
Midnight Madness - *Pulled Up*	10.10-5	M. Richards	25/1
Bucko - *Pulled Up*	11.10-5	M. Dwyer	16/1
Strands Of Gold - *Fell*	9.10-3	P. Scudamore	20/1
Gee-A - *Pulled Up*	9.10-3	Gee Armytage	33/1
You're Welcome - *Pulled Up*	12.10-1	P. Hobbs	33/1
Repington - *Refused*	10.10-1	C. Hawkins	16/1
Tracys Special - *Pulled Up*	11.10-0	S.C. Knight	33/1
Sacred Path - *Fell*	8.10-0	C. Cox	17/2*
Memberson - *Pulled Up*	10.10-3	R.J. Beggan	33/1
Northern Bay - *Pulled Up*	12.10-4	H. Davies	50/1
Sir Jest - *Refused*	10.10-2	K. Jones	22/1
Kumbi - *Fell*	13.10-0	C. Llewellyn	100/1
Smith's Man - *Pulled Up*	10.10-0	M. Perrett	50/1
Big Brown Bear - *Refused*	11.10-2	R. Stronge	66/1
Bright Dream - *Brought Down*	12.10-2	R. Rowe	66/1
Insure - *Unseated Rider*	10.10-0	B. De Haan	80/1
Lastofthebrownies - *Fell*	8.10-0	T. Carmody	25/1
Eton Rouge - *Pulled Up*	9.10-5	D. Browne	25/1
Marcolo - *Fell*	11.10-0	Miss V. Williams	200/1
Polly's Pal	10.10-0	J.K. Kinane	100/1
- *Jockey Knocked From Saddle*			
Smartside - *Fell*	13.10-4	Mr A. Hambly	100/1
Brass Change - *Fell*	10.10-0	M. Kinane	100/1
Preben Fur - *Pulled Up*	11.10-0	S.J. O'Neill	100/1
Tullamarine - *Fell*	11.10-0	M. Bowlby	200/1
Seeandem - *Refused*	8.10-0	P. Leech	100/1
Oyde Hills - *Refused*	9.10-0	M. Brennan	100/1
Hettinger - *Fell*	8.10-0	Penny Ffitch-Heyes	200/1

Rhyme 'N' Reason became the toast of his stable after staging one of the most amazing recoveries of all time.

1989
LITTLE POLVEIR

It is often the case that the Cheltenham Festival, which normally precedes the Grand National by around three weeks, unveils or highlights potential challengers for the big race at Aintree. Horses that can power up the tough and demanding finishing hill at Cheltenham are usually considered ideal candidates for the National.

This formula was again followed for the 1989 Grand National, when the lightly raced ten-year-old Dixton House was made favourite for the race. With leg injuries resulting in two years off the track, Dixton House was participating in only his second comeback race when he destroyed his opponents in the Ritz Club Chase at Cheltenham to prove his fitness. Trained by John Edwards and ridden by Tom Morgan, the horse arrived at Aintree fresh and lightly weighted and, with ground conditions in his favour, a bold showing was expected.

Holding a particularly strong hand on this occasion was the northern-based trainer Arthur Stephenson, with Durham Edition and The Thinker the spearheads for his team of four. Trained specifically for the National, Durham Edition held second place in the market and had not risen by a great deal in the weights after his strong performance of a year ago. The majestic eleven-year-old The Thinker entered the race as top weight, having won the 1987 Cheltenham Gold Cup, and was unquestionably the classiest horse in the field. Having had a reasonably light campaign, The Thinker had won his first two races of the season before suffering a rare fall early on as he attempted to recapture his Gold Cup crown. The horse also had proven stamina, being a former winner of the Midlands Grand National. Rounding out Stephenson's team were a pair of useful outsiders, the consistent Sir Jest and the Eider Chase winner Polar Nomad.

Considered by some to be too small a horse to cope with the daunting Aintree fences, there was no doubting the ability of the tiny Martin Pipe runner, Bonanza Boy. A mud-lover, Bonanza Boy had won the Welsh Grand National earlier in the season and had also finished a creditable fourth to the great Desert Orchid in the Cheltenham Gold Cup. With Peter Scudamore on board and testing conditions lying in wait, the Aintree first-timer was backed heavily on the eve of the race, eventually starting at 10/1.

With seven Grand National runs between them, West Tip and Little Polveir were undoubtedly the Aintree veterans of the line-up, yet the two had experienced contrasting results in previous Nationals. West Tip had comfortably won the race in 1986 and had run superbly in the next two editions, but Little Polveir had not completed the course since trailing home a distant ninth the year West Tip triumphed. It was not surprising then that West Tip, who had won his first race since his finest hour in a hunter-chase at Hereford earlier in the season, was by far the more fancied of the two at 12/1. However, some shrewd punters had recalled just how strongly Little Polveir was going before unseating his rider five fences from home in last season's race, and although the former Scottish Grand National winner was available at 50/1 on the morning of the race, thirty-year-old Jimmy Frost's first ride in the event started at 28/1.

Stearsby, Perris Valley and Smart Tar were three exciting newcomers to the race. Brendan Powell was looking for his second consecutive winning National ride and, in Stearsby, he had a horse that had won his last race easily at Nottingham and was a former winner of the Welsh Grand National. Also in cracking form was the Irish challenger Perris Valley, following a recent win at Leopardstown, and Dermot Weld's charge, who had won the Irish Grand National the season before, was running in the same colours as Aintree legend Greasepaint, while trainer Mark Wilkinson's first runner in the race, Smart Tar, carried the famous Courage colours which had been so splendidly represented by Spanish Steps in the 1970s.

Having fallen at the first fence the year before, and a total outsider on this occasion, the chancy-jumping Hettinger was the subject of an interesting challenge. The horse, ridden by Ray Goldstein, was set to earn £200 from bookmakers Victor Chandler if he cleared the first fence, and £100 for every fence thereafter. All the money raised would be presented to the Leukaemia Research Fund.

With the bright sunshine drying out the softened ground to a degree, the forty runners were forced to wait to begin their bids for glory. First, Memberson spread a plate which caused a delay and just as they were at last ready to go, the temperamental ten-year-old Bob Tisdall surged through the starting tape, leaving it requiring repairs.

To a belated roar, the runners were finally sent on their way, but even then the decidedly weak-looking tape sprayed in front of the path of those on the outside as they charged off. Bob Tisdall, continuing his stubbornness, refused to jump off with the others and, when he did eventually get going, he was a fence behind the rest of the field.

With Brown Trix on the far outside and West Tip in the centre leading the way, the runners hit the first fence bathed in glorious sun, but Cerimau, representing David Elsworth's stable, hit the deck straight away, followed by Cranlome at the second.

Brown Trix lost some ground after a hesitant jump at the big ditch and Stearsby took his place in the lead. The favourite, Dixton House, had pulled his way to the front in the centre of the course with West Tip, Newnham and Mithras travelling strongly down the inside, and that was how the leaders remained as they hurtled down to Becher's Brook.

The race was about to take a dramatic twist, as Dixton House rose to take the monstrous fence in the lead. Losing his footing on the landing side, the favourite sprawled over to exit the race in agonising fashion. Further back, a pair of horrific accidents took place that would ultimately change the stature of Becher's forever. Both Brown Trix and Seeandem crashed through the fence, hit the sloping ground and ended up in the brook in disturbing fatal falls. Amidst all the drama, Hettinger's fundraising bid had met its end, the grey Sergeant Sprite had fallen and Sir Jest had been brought down in the confusion.

Racing away from these vicious incidents, Stearsby and West Tip began to exhibit some spectacular leaps out in front until Stearsby bluntly refused at the eleventh, sending Brendan Powell flying over the top of the fence. Now out on his own in front, West Tip proudly led a big group back onto the racecourse, with Newnham, Team Challenge, Little Polveir, Mr Chris, Smart Tar, Kersil and Mithras the closest to him.

In a perfect line over the Chair, Little Polveir, Mithras, West Tip and Kersil brought roars from the crowd with some bold jumping, but the fourteen-year-old Smartside departed the race, while Mr Chris tripped and somersaulted in crazy fashion after clearing the Water.

During the early part of the second circuit, Smart Tar had constructed a run down the outside, which was appearing increasingly threatening with every jump, but when a mistake sent Carl Llewellyn shooting from the saddle at the twentieth, his hopes were wrecked, and it was Little Polveir, just like the year before, that led the race as it entered its serious stage.

The original racecard from the 1989 edition.

As they came to Becher's again, there were still plenty in contention, including West Tip, Lastofthebrownies, Monanore, Team Challenge and the rapidly improving pair of Bonanza Boy and Durham Edition; fortunately, there was no repeat of the earlier drama at the fence.

Jumping every fence down the back with increased confidence, Little Polveir still held the lead with a relentless gallop, but as they crossed the Melling Road for a final time, nine horses, with The Thinker staying on strongly, had still not been eliminated, setting up an enthralling finish.

Travelling best of all was Durham Edition, and as Little Polveir belted the last fence, taking numerous branches of spruce with him, Chris Grant's mount looked as though he would scream away on the flat. But, just like the season before, Durham Edition had not been able to quicken on the run-in, and joined by the rider-less Smart Tar, Little Polveir found another spurt of energy to resume command at the elbow.

Shooting past Durham Edition, West Tip and The Thinker emerged from the pack to challenge the leader and, at one point, looked to be catching him. It was not to be though as, helped by the loose horse, Little Polveir surged away again to record a surprising but thoroughly deserved victory by seven lengths.

The runner-up West Tip had battled back in to the picture, having been outpaced two from home, to confirm his love affair with Aintree, while The Thinker had displayed tremendous heart under a heavy burden to take third. Having faded badly up the run-in, the unfortunate Durham Edition was caught for fourth by the Irish horse Lastofthebrownies.

Little Polveir had made up for missing a winning opportunity in 1988 by holding off all his challengers with a brave display of front running, and the horse that was named after a salmon pool on the River Dee could now take his place on the Grand National roll of honour, after achieving victory at the fourth attempt.

Winning trainer Toby Balding, who had sent out Highland Wedding for National glory twenty years earlier, had only been sent the horse after owner Mr Ted Harvey had bought Little Polveir for his son David to ride in amateur events six weeks before the National. Balding was quick to deflect credit on to John Edwards, who had previously trained the horse and, ironically, was out of luck on this occasion with the race favourite Dixton House.

Winning jockey Jimmy Frost had clearly done his homework on Little Polveir, as he had studied footage of the 1988 race in an attempt to improve the horse's chances on this occasion, and he was gloriously rewarded with an inspired win on the twelve-year-old.

Following the sad episodes at Becher's Brook, calls to radically change the layout of the obstacle were numerous, while Labour MP Tony Banks even put forward the exaggerated notion in the House of Commons for the race to be banned. The Jockey Club's response was to conduct a full investigation into the race's safety. As a result, Becher's was drastically altered some months later, with the notorious brook filled in and the slope on the landing slide levelled off considerably.

HORSE/FATE	AGE/WEIGHT	JOCKEY	ODDS
1st LITTLE POLVEIR	12.10-3	J. FROST	28/1
2nd WEST TIP	12.10-11	R. DUNWOODY	12/1
3rd THE THINKER	11.11-10	S. SHERWOOD	10/1
4th LASTOFTHEBROWNIES	9.10-0	T. CARMODY	16/1
5th Durham Edition	11.10-11	C. Grant	15/2
6th Monanore	12.10-6	G. McCourt	20/1
7th Gala's Image	9.10-3	N. Doughty	18/1
8th Bonanza Boy	8.11-1	P. Scudamore	10/1
9th Team Challenge	7.10-0	M. Bowlby	30/1
10th Newnham	12.10-5	Mr S. Andrews	50/1
11th The Thirsty Farmer	10.10-2	L. Kelp	100/1
12th Attitude Adjuster	9.10-6	N. Madden	25/1
13th Sidbury Hill	13.10-0	K. Mooney	100/1
14th Mr Baker	11.10-0	M. Moran	100/1
Stearsby - *Refused*	10.10-9	B. Powell	14/1
Bob Tisdall - *Refused*	10.10-7	J. White	25/1
Smart Tar - *Fell*	8.10-3	C. Llewellyn	18/1
Dixton House - *Fell*	10.10-3	T. Morgan	7/1*
Perris Valley - *Fell*	8.10-0	B. Sheridan	16/1
Gainsay - *Fell*	10.10-6	M. Pitman	25/1
Memberson - *Pulled Up*	11.10-2	Mr G. Upton	33/1
Cranlome - *Fell*	11.10-0	K.F. O'Brien	66/1
Sir Jest - *Brought Down*	11.10-1	M. Hammond	40/1
Queensway Boy - *Refused*	10.10-0	A. Webb	50/1
Beamwam - *Pulled Up*	11.10-6	Mr D. Naylor-Leyland	100/1
Sergeant Sprite - *Fell*	9.10-2	T.J. Taafe	50/1
Bartres - *Pulled Up*	10.10-3	G. Bradley	33/1
Brown Trix - *Fell*	11.10-5	Mr D.F. Pitcher	300/1
Seeandem - *Fell*	9.10-0	L. Cusack	100/1
Cerimau - *Fell*	11.10-0	P. Hobbs	80/1
Rausal - *Refused*	10.10-0	D. Tegg	50/1
Friendly Henry - *Fell*	9.10-4	H. Davies	66/1
Mithras - *Pulled Up*	11.10-1	R. Stronge	66/1
Polar Nomad - *Pulled Up*	8.10-0	A. Merrigan	80/1
Numerate - *Pulled Up*	10.10-0	Tarnya Davis	100/1
Hettinger - *Fell*	9.10-0	R. Goldstein	300/1
Kersil - *Pulled Up*	12.10-0	A. Orkney	300/1
Mearlin - *Pulled Up*	10.10-0	S. McNeill	300/1
Smartside - *Refused*	14.10-5	Mr A. Hambly	300/1
Mr Chris - *Fell*	10.10-0	B. Storey	200/1

1990
MR FRISK

With the much publicised modifications to several of the Grand National fences, the 1990 running found itself heavily in the spotlight as critics of the event waited to see if the changes would have a positive affect on the general safety of the race. The most notable differences were at the once beastly Becher's Brook. Although it still presented a formidable challenge to horse and rider, gone was the treacherous sloping drop on the landing side which had caused so many problems, and in its place was a more even, gradual descent to the now filled-in brook.

A racegoer standing in the new-look Becher's Brook – showing that the obstacle still presents a formidable challenge.

With an extended dry spell leading up to the race, the ground on this occasion was extremely fast, and while this was unsuitable for Sacred Path and Why So Hasty, who were both pulled out on the morning of the race, there were plenty of others who were going to relish the conditions.

One of those was the Nicky Henderson-trained eight-year-old Brown Windsor, who was rapidly developing into one of the finest chasers in the land. Having won the Whitbread Gold Cup as a novice, Brown Windsor had confirmed his improvement during the season and had only narrowly been beaten in the Hennessy Gold Cup by another National contender in Ghofar, while more recently he had impressively won the Cathcart Chase at the Cheltenham Festival. Henderson and jockey John White had taken second in the 1987 National with The Tsarevich, and having never fallen over fences, Brown Windsor was sent off the 7/1 favourite to go one better for the stable.

Having been travelling like a winner in the closing stages of the last two Nationals but failing to come out on top, many people believed that the fast ground would help Durham Edition finally emerge victorious this time. The horse had won twice at Wetherby earlier in the season, before being given a break in the build-up to the race. Once more ridden by Chris Grant, a victory would prove the perfect seventieth-birthday present for trainer Arthur Stephenson.

Listed together at 16/1 were another pair of fast-ground lovers, Mr Frisk and Uncle Merlin. Pulled out on the eve of the 1989 Grand National due to unsuitably soft going, Kim Bailey's runner, Mr Frisk, was expected to thrive on the Aintree surface this time. Having won at Ascot in November, Mr Frisk had enjoyed a consistent season and was to be ridden by stylish amateur Marcus Armytage. The exciting jumper from America, Uncle Merlin, was naturally compared to the National winner of 1980, Ben Nevis, for he too was a former winner of the Maryland Hunt Cup and was also in training with Captain Tim Forster. With a win at Wincanton in January behind him, Uncle Merlin had the considerable experience of Hywel Davies in the saddle.

Bigsun, Rinus and Call Collect each attracted their fair share of attention in the betting market. Bigsun – a horse that Richard Dunwoody had deserted long-time Aintree partner West Tip for – had won over four miles at Cheltenham earlier in the season and had then shot towards the head of the National market with a fine win in the Ritz Club Chase at the Cheltenham Festival. The lightly-raced Rinus was looking to give trainer Gordon Richards a third Grand National win and had won his latest outing at Haydock Park, while Call Collect had won Foxhunter Chases at both Aintree and Cheltenham and clearly had talent in abundance, although trainer John Parkes had been openly concerned about running his horse on the big day, fearing he would not handle the fast ground.

With Aintree basking in sunshine, Polyfemus delayed the start of the race when he had to be re-plated. Then, with the eyes of the world on them, the thirty-eight runners were unleashed, charging away at a terrific pace.

The bold-running two-mile specialist Star's Delight, with Jonathon Lower on board, led explosively to the first fence on the wide outside, with Polyfemus parallel to him on the inside; Gala's Image was the only one to be caught out at the opener. It was not long before the American challenger Uncle Merlin had joined the leaders, and soaring the big ditch, he was bowling along in the middle of the track with Brown Windsor, Mr Frisk, Gee-A and Charter Hardware keeping him company, but further back Conclusive and Thinking Cap dropped out of the race.

There was a huge sense of anticipation as the field came to the new-look Becher's Brook for the first time, led by Uncle Merlin and Mr Frisk, and jumping it boldly, the leaders surged onwards. The famous fence proved it still retained an element of bite by claiming Lanavoe, but more importantly, the veteran Young Driver, who went lame jumping the obstacle, avoided more serious injury due to the decreased risks it now offered – for which his jockey Jimmy Duggan was particularly grateful.

It was with bitter irony then that, with the fence that had been the cause for such criticism from some quarters safely negotiated, it would be the Canal Turn that would provide a terribly sad moment in the race. With Uncle Merlin and Mr Frisk still tearing away in front, the previous year's Scottish Grand National winner Roll-A-Joint plunged headfirst to the ground and broke his neck in a horrific fall.

The lead was still held with authority by Uncle Merlin and Mr Frisk as they jumped the fences out in the country, with Brown Windsor, Polyfemus and the quirky grey horse Pukka Major in close pursuit.

Star's Delight, who had earlier lost huge amounts of ground by jumping very wide at the Canal Turn, was pulled up before the thirteenth fence, while at the next, Gainsay crashed to an ugly fall and, on struggling to his feet, collided with the tailed-off Aintree stalwart Monanore, sending him through the protective barriers.

In third place jumping the Chair, Polyfemus ripped through the top of the obstacle and knocked the stuffing out of himself in the process, while at the back of the field, Huntworth's back legs clipped the obstacle, causing him to tumble to the ground.

The fast ground and electric pace were taking their toll on a number of the runners and, as the field set off for the second circuit, those left in the race were distinctly strung out, with Bonanza Boy, West Tip and Call Collect all struggling at the rear of the pack.

Enjoying themselves and jumping like stags out in front, Uncle Merlin and Mr Frisk were matching each other stride for stride as they advanced their lead over the rest. Back in the field, the retreating Irish runner Hungary Hur tragically became the race's second fatality after shattering a leg on the run to the big ditch.

Of the two leaders, Uncle Merlin appeared to be gaining the upper hand, and with another spectacular jump, he developed a slight advantage as he came to take Becher's. Sailing over in majestic fashion, the American horse landed steeply and staggered on landing, dislodging a distraught Hywel Davies from the saddle. Although it was still a long way to the finish, Uncle Merlin had given no indication of tiring and, with only a featherweight to shoulder, he could be considered desperately unlucky.

Not that this mattered to Mr Frisk, who had also been jumping superbly and was now left on his own. Marcus Armytage sent him in to every fence down the back in thrilling and attacking style, with only Rinus, Sir Jest, Brown Windsor and Durham Edition anywhere in the vicinity.

Two fences from home, only three had a chance of winning, and with Mr Frisk appearing to tire, Rinus was not far behind. However, yet again Chris Grant had coasted

Durham Edition through to challenge menacingly, and by the final flight, he and Mr Frisk had the race to themselves.

When Mr Frisk brushed through the last, Durham Edition bounded up smoothly on his shoulder and finally looked ready to capture that elusive Aintree victory and bury the ghosts of Nationals past. Up the final run-in, both horses were giving their all, but in one of the most polished riding finishes in recent memory, the amateur Marcus Armytage masterfully coaxed Mr Frisk to another effort and his mount responded in resilient style to hold the luckless Durham Edition by under a length.

Punching the air in triumph, Armytage became the first amateur to win since Dick Saunders in 1982, sealing a fabulous victory in which Mr Frisk had led for most of the way on the blazing fast ground and subsequently shattered the course record, set by Red Rum in 1973, by over fourteen seconds.

Chris Grant had now finished second an agonising three times, twice on Durham Edition, and had unfortunately been out-battled up the long run-in once again. Rinus had come home well in third, maintaining jockey Neale Doughty's one hundred percent record in the race, with Brown Windsor narrowly denying Lastofthebrownies fourth.

Having run in every Grand National since 1985 and 1986 respectively, it was announced after the race that West Tip and Monanore, two grand servants to the event, had run their final Nationals. Although Monanore was carried out of the race at the fourteenth, West Tip came home as gamely as ever in tenth.

As expected, there was further disapproval following the loss of two more brave horses, yet it was noticeable that Becher's Brook this time avoided any controversy.

Realising that, at eighty-two years of age, she was not getting any younger, American owner Mrs Harry Duffey had given permission for her beloved Mr Frisk to try his luck in the National, having previously been reluctant to risk him; she was rewarded with a breathtaking victory from her prized chestnut.

Having trained his first Grand National winner, jubilant trainer Kim Bailey automatically set his sights on a repeat victory with Mr Frisk in twelve months' time.

HORSE/FATE	AGE/WEIGHT	JOCKEY	ODDS
1st **MR FRISK**	11.10-6	MR M. ARMYTAGE	16/1
2nd **DURHAM EDITION**	12.10-9	C. GRANT	9/1
3rd **RINUS**	9.10-4	N. DOUGHTY	13/1
4th **BROWN WINDSOR**	8.10-10	J. WHITE	7/1*
5th Lastofthebrownies	10.10-0	C.F. Swan	20/1
6th Bigsun	9.10-2	R. Dunwoody	15/2
7th Call Collect	9.10-5	Mr R. Martin	14/1
8th Bartres	11.10-0	M. Bowlby	66/1
9th Sir Jest	12.10-0	B. Storey	66/1
10th West Tip	13.10-11	P. Hobbs	20/1
11th Team Challenge	8.10-0	B. De Haan	50/1
12th Charter Hardware	8.10-0	N. Williamson	66/1
13th Gallic Prince	11.10-4	Mr J.F. Simo	100/1
14th Ghofar	7.10-0	B. Powell	14/1
15th Course Hunter	12.10-0	G. Bradley	66/1
16th Bonanza Boy	9.11-9	P. Scudamore	16/1
17th Solares	10.10-0	Mr P. McMahon	150/1
18th Gee-A	11.10-2	D.J. Murphy	66/1
19th Mick's Star	10.10-1	S.J. O'Neill	66/1
20th Bob Tisdall	11.10-5	K. Mooney	66/1
Hungary Hur - *Pulled Up*	11.11-2	T. Carmody	50/1
Pukka Major - *Unseated Rider*	9.10-4	M. Richards	100/1
Gainsay - *Fell*	11.10-7	M. Pitman	66/1
Joint Sovereignty - *Unseated Rider*	10.10-1	L. Wyer	50/1
Monanore - *Carried Out*	13.10-5	T.J. Taafe	100/1
Star's Delight - *Pulled Up*	8.10-0	J. Lower	50/1
Gala's Image - *Fell*	10.10-0	J. Shortt	66/1
Torside - *Pulled Up*	11.10-3	J. Frost	66/1
Roll-A-Joint - *Fell*	12.10-0	S. McNeill	28/1
Polyfemus - *Pulled Up*	8.10-2	R. Rowe	18/1
Conclusive - *Fell*	11.10-4	S. Smith-Eccles	28/1
Nautical Joke - *Unseated Rider*	11.10-0	Mr K. Johnson	66/1
Against The Grain - *Pulled Up*	9.10-0	J. Osborne	25/1
Young Driver - *Pulled Up*	13.10-4	J. Duggan	150/1
Uncle Merlin - *Unseated Rider*	9.10-3	H. Davies	16/1
Lanavoe - *Fell*	11.10-0	P. Leech	100/1
Huntworth - *Fell*	10.10-9	Mr A. Walter	66/1
Thinking Cap - *Fell*	9.10-0	P. Malone	100/1

1991
SEAGRAM

No horse had won the Cheltenham Gold Cup and the Grand National in the same season since Golden Miller in 1934. In recent times, Davy Lad and Alverton had both attempted to win both races, but had been unsuccessful. In the 1991 Grand National, Jenny Pitman, already a winner with Corbiere in 1983, put forward a very realistic contender to try and capture the elusive double.

The horse was the striking eight-year-old Garrison Savannah, whom Mrs Pitman had guided through a chasing career littered with injuries to win the Gold Cup the previous month on only his second run of the season. With a relatively light racing weight for a Gold Cup winner of 11st 1lb and with the trainer's son Mark in the saddle, Garrison Savannah was a hugely popular choice at 7/1.

Due to rain pounding down on Aintree during the week, the favourite on the day was Martin Pipe's dual Welsh Grand National winner, Bonanza Boy. The horse had enjoyed a consistent season, and arrived at Aintree having won over four miles at Uttoxeter recently. Bonanza Boy had disappointed when finishing unplaced in the previous two Nationals, but with conditions in his favour and Peter Scudamore on board, he clearly had a favourite's chance this time round and started at 13/2.

Conversely, the ground was only just deemed reasonable enough for last year's hero Mr Frisk to take part. Trainer Kim Bailey had threatened to pull the horse out if the ground became too soft, but he was eventually allowed to take his chance. The horse had begun his repeat-National campaign well, with a pair of victories, but after a puzzling defeat on his latest start, together with increased weight and a lack of fast ground, Mr Frisk faded in the betting market, eventually starting at 25/1.

With a light, successful campaign behind him and ideally weighted for the race, Rinus was another very popular choice on the day. Trained by Gordon Richards especially for the National, the horse had yet to fall in thirty-two races over fences and ground conditions were certainly in his favour on this occasion. In Neale Doughty, Rinus had a jockey who was fast developing a reputation for being the Aintree specialist, as he had completed the course during all seven of his rides in the race, and having guided Hallo Dandy to victory in 1984, confidence was high that the Welshman could work similar magic this time.

Having his first ride in the Grand National was Nigel Hawke on the tough, New Zealand-bred chaser Seagram. Trained by David Barons, Seagram had enjoyed a particularly consistent season in which he was regularly in amongst the prize money. On his latest run at the Cheltenham Festival, the horse had entered many Aintree notebooks with a comfortable success in the Ritz Club Chase and, sharing the same name as the race sponsors, Seagram proved a common choice for punters and started at 12/1.

Docklands Express, Ballyhane and Durham Edition all had their followers on the day. Ultra-consistent, and a recent winner of the valuable Racing Post Chase at Kempton Park, Docklands Express was seen by many as a more likely winner for Kim Bailey this time than Mr Frisk, while Ballyhane had been an encouraging third behind Docklands Express at Kempton, and was one of four good horses representing Josh Gifford's stable, the others being Envopak Token, Foyle Fisherman and Golden Minstrel. Although he was thirteen now, Durham Edition deserved a Grand National more than most, having run three fine races at Aintree, while a victory would prove the perfect tonic for his trainer, Arthur Stephenson, who had lost his star chaser and leading National contender The Thinker in a freak work accident two days before the race.

With the Czechoslovakian mare Fraze and the French-trained runner Oklaoma II giving the race a true international feel, the forty runners assembled at the start and prepared for their assault on glory. They were unfortunately made to wait, however, as first, Nicky Henderson's runner Ten Of Spades spread a plate, and then animal rights protestors thought it would be a good idea to irritate the horses some more by running on to the course brandishing abusive banners.

As the track was cleared for the runners to be allowed on their way at last, an enormous cheer went up from the spectators, and it was the headstrong Oklaoma II who thundered down the inside to lead at the first fence. Towards the outside, Docklands Express, who had never finished outside the first three in fourteen runs over fences,

The splendid Garrison Savannah clears the last – apparently on the way to a historic Gold Cup/Grand National double ...

... until Nigel Hawke and Seagram snatch victory in a thrilling climax.

had his streak ended abruptly as he fell, giving jockey Anthony Tory a rude introduction to the National.

Leaving behind the fallen Run And Skip at the second, Golden Freeze led the tightly-packed field down to Becher's Brook with Mr Frisk travelling well on the outside with Over The Road, while French raider Oklaoma II continued up with the pace on the inside.

Taming Becher's in great style, Golden Freeze led the march out into the country, where for the first time, the well-fancied Rinus leapt into contention at Valentine's Brook, and although the twelfth fence claimed outsider Joint Sovereignty, the lead remained virtually unchanged as the field swung back onto the racecourse proper.

Powering towards the big Chair fence, Golden Freeze and jockey Michael Bowlby continued to rattle along in front, and as the leader came to the famous obstacle, stable-mates Team Challenge and Garrison Savannah, the latter having breezed into contention after one circuit, joined him.

With the usual colourful and enthusiastic showering of applause and encouragement, the field raced away from the grandstand and into the distance to begin their final circuit, with the lead still held by Golden Freeze; following him came Team Challenge, Oklaoma II, Rinus, Garrison Savannah, General Chandos, Ballyhane and Over The Road. At this stage, Bonanza Boy had a lot of ground to make up on the leaders, while Mr Frisk was starting to struggle and was soon heading backwards.

Right in the middle of the track, Rinus was delivering a bold bid for honours and, two fences before Becher's, he jumped to the fore. However, after scraping the top of the fence, he came down to a shocked reaction from the crowd and was out of the race.

This now left a group that began to make a distinct move for glory. It was Golden Freeze that still led, but Garrison Savannah was cruising on the inside, with Seagram improving all the time, while New Halen, Auntie Dot, Over The Road and Durham Edition were still in the hunt as they came to Becher's again. New Halen, a 50/1 outsider, was starting to make impressive progress when a bad blunder at the Brook had him brushing his nose on the turf, while further back, Blue Dart's mistake resulted in the unseating of Hywel Davies and Bigsun also blundered away his faint hopes.

A tremendous roar echoed round Aintree as Garrison Savannah leapt to the front at the Foinavon fence, and from then on he commanded the lead on the inside, seemingly destined to join the great winning horses that have graced Aintree. Jumping every fence like a buck, the Gold Cup winner oozed class running down the back and as they reached the turn for home, his nearest pursuers – Auntie Dot, Seagram, Durham Edition and Over The Road – were all struggling to stay with him.

Jumping the final two fences with fluid accuracy, Garrison Savannah had shaken off all but Seagram, and even he was some way adrift as Mark Pitman's mount bounded clear up the run-in, and was between eight and ten lengths clear at the elbow.

Just as the historic double had looked a certainty, Garrison Savannah began to tire dramatically, and under a relentless charge summoned by Hawke, Seagram started to cut away at the lead. In ferocious style, Seagram powered past the now leg-weary Garrison Savannah and Hawke flung his arm towards the sky as he crossed the winning line five lengths in front.

Garrison Savannah had given everything he had. The horse had jumped beautifully and Mark Pitman had given him a superb ride. In the end, however, a combination of extra weight, stamina-sapping ground and an extremely strong finishing burst by Seagram had denied him a historic victory, and the horse had succumbed in much the same way that Crisp had to Red Rum for Mark's father, Richard, in 1973.

The mare Auntie Dot had travelled exceptionally well on the final lap until fading to finish third, while Over The Road just held the fast-finishing favourite Bonanza Boy and the gallant Durham Edition for fourth. The one sad note to a fantastic Grand National was the loss of the game Ballyhane, who suffered a haemorrhage ten minutes after the race.

The brave, battling qualities of Seagram had provided trainer David Barons and jockey Nigel Hawke with a monumental victory, and the horse had displayed a vast amount of courage to overturn Garrison Savannah's seemingly unsurpassable lead in the closing stages.

For Major Ivan Straker, the chief of race sponsors Seagram, the only frustrating aspect to another hugely successful Grand National was the knowledge that on two occasions he had been offered Sir Eric Parker's big race hero, and both times had declined to purchase the now triumphant eleven-year-old.

With no fatalities over the National fences themselves, RSPCA members were to demonstrate their pleasure with the modified fences, but had urged all concerned that it was still far too early to classify the 1989 changes as an ultimate success.

HORSE/FATE		AGE/WEIGHT	JOCKEY	ODDS
1st	SEAGRAM	11.10-6	N. HAWKE	12/1
2nd	GARRISON SAVANNAH	8.11-1	M. PITMAN	7/1
3rd	AUNTIE DOT	10.10-4	M. DWYER	50/1
4th	OVER THE ROAD	10.10-0	R. SUPPLE	50/1
5th	Bonanza Boy	10.11-7	P. Scudamore	13/2*
6th	Durham Edition	13.10-13	C. Grant	25/1
7th	Golden Minstrel	12.10-2	T. Grantham	50/1
8th	Old Applejack	11.10-1	T. Reed	66/1
9th	Leagaune	9.10-0	M. Richards	200/1
10th	Foyle Fisherman	12.10-0	E. Murphy	40/1
11th	Ballyhane	10.10-3	D. Murphy	22/1
12th	Harley	11.10-0	G. Lyons	150/1
13th	Mick's Star	11.10-0	C. Swan	100/1
14th	Ten Of Spades	11.11-1	J. White	15/1
15th	Forest Ranger	9.10-0	D. Tegg	100/1
16th	Yahoo	10.11-1	N. Williamson	33/1
17th	Golden Freeze	9.11-0	M. Bowlby	40/1
Fraze - *Pulled Up*		8.11-10	V. Chaloupka	100/1
Mr Frisk - *Pulled Up*		12.11-6	Mr M. Armytage	25/1
Rinus - *Fell*		10.10-7	N. Doughty	7/1
Oklaoma II - *Pulled Up*		11.10-7	R. Kleparski	66/1
Master Bob - *Pulled Up*		11.10-5	J. Osborne	20/1
Bigsun - *Pulled Up*		10.10-4	R. Dunwoody	9/1
Solidasarock - *Pulled Up*		9.10-4	G. Bradley	50/1
Docklands Express - *Fell*		9.10-3	A. Tory	20/1
Huntworth - *Pulled Up*		11.10-8	Mr A. Walter	50/1
Crammer - *Unseated Rider*		11.10-2	Mr J. Durkan	28/1
Southernair - *Fell*		11.10-1	Mr J. Simo	100/1
Envopak Token - *Pulled Up*		10.10-0	M. Perrett	28/1
New Halen - *Unseated Rider*		10.10-0	S.J. O'Neill	50/1
Run And Skip - *Fell*		13.10-0	D. Byrne	66/1
General Chandos - *Pulled Up*		10.10-3	Mr J. Bradburne	150/1
The Langholm Dyer - *Unseated Rider*		12.10-6	G. McCourt	100/1
Team Challenge - *Refused*		9.10-0	B. De Haan	50/1
Joint Sovereignty - *Fell*		11.10-0	L. O'Hara	100/1
Bumbles Folly - *Pulled Up*		10.10-5	J. Frost	150/1
Mister Christian -*Pulled Up*		10.10-0	S. Earle	100/1
Hotplate - *Pulled Up*		8.10-2	P. Niven	80/1
Blue Dart - *Unseated Rider*		11.10-2	H. Davies	80/1
Abba Lad - *Pulled Up*		9.10-0	D. Gallagher	250/1

1992
PARTY POLITICS

With Seagram fittingly winning the last Seagram Grand National the year before, the hugely successful race sponsors passed the mantle on to one of their products, Martell Cognac, and so the 1992 race became the first Martell Grand National.

As in the previous season, the Cheltenham Gold Cup winner from the preceding month graced the National with his presence. On this occasion, the horse was the combative stayer Cool Ground from the yard of Toby Balding, trainer of previous National winners Highland Wedding and Little Polveir. Also a winner of the Welsh Grand National, the ten-year-old had endured a strenuous, but ultimately victorious, battle up the Cheltenham hill with the French horse The Fellow and another Grand National runner, Docklands Express. With his regular partner, the brilliant youngster Adrian Maguire, missing through injury, Martin Lynch received a dream spare ride on the chestnut. Looking to go one better than Garrison Savannah in 1991, Cool Ground had a decent weight of 11st 1lb, and was predictably high in the betting at 10/1.

Perhaps it was the absence of the testing conditions and the heavy ground preferred by the Gold Cup winner that resulted in other horses being marginally

more fancied on this occasion. The horse that was eventually to start favourite was Docklands Express, a first fence casualty in the previous year's race. The horse had won a Whitbread Gold Cup on a disqualification at the end of the previous season and, during the current campaign, had displayed remarkable consistency to finish among the places in the Hennessy Gold Cup, King George VI Chase and the Cheltenham Gold Cup. With Peter Scudamore booked to replace the injured Anthony Tory, and with a number of dry days leading up to the race, Docklands Express attracted a huge amount of support to top the market on 15/2.

At the head of the weights for the race were Twin Oaks and the defending champion Seagram. Trained by Gordon Richards, the impressively built chaser

Twin Oaks had recorded six wins over the awkward Haydock Park fences in his career and was used to shouldering big weights, while his jockey Neale Doughty had suffered his only ever fall in the race the previous year on Rinus. For Seagram though, the season had proved disappointing. The twelve-year-old now had a much heftier burden of 11st 4lb to carry and was largely unfancied in the betting at 33/1.

Having missed a season through injury, Nicky Henderson's Brown Windsor arrived at Aintree in good form having won his latest race at Sandown Park. The horse had run well in the 1990 Grand National and conditions were turning in his favour on this occasion. With the added assistance of Richard Dunwoody in the saddle, the horse held a prominent position in the market at 8/1.

Just as they had before the 1986 National, the Cheveley Park Stud owners, David and Patricia Thompson, swooped to acquire a pair of challengers for the big race, this time to run in Mrs Thompson's pink and purple silks. The two were Party Politics and Roc De Prince. While the latter was a relative outsider, the giant Party Politics became a very topical selection with the country in an election year. Standing over eighteen hands high, Party Politics had been runner-up in both the Hennessy Gold Cup and the Welsh Grand National, but his latest two runs had proved somewhat disappointing. Even so, with Carl Llewellyn standing in for the injured Andy Adams, the thorough stayer was listed just after the principals in the betting at 14/1.

Other horses to attract interest in a fiercely competitive field were Auntie Dot, Laura's Beau, Romany King and Stay On Tracks. The mare Auntie Dot had long been among the favourites for the National after travelling well for a long way before fading to finish third the previous year, while Irish raider Laura's Beau was owned by J.P. McManus, and the colourful character had placed a considerable bet on his horse finishing in the places. Romany King was another horse representing trainer Toby Balding, and was an improving eight-year-old who had won three races earlier in the season, while Arthur Stephenson hoped the grey Stay On Tracks, who had been third in the Eider Chase, would carry on the brilliant National sequence set by Durham Edition.

With no problems holding up the start this year, the field broke away and approached the first fence at an even pace. As Josh Gifford's veteran runner Golden Minstrel led on the inside from Ghofar in the centre, Rawhide became the only casualty at the opener after unseating Kevin O'Brien. Ghofar made a shocking mistake at the big ditch but survived, and as they neared Becher's Brook, he was in a leading bunch that included Golden Minstrel, Forest Ranger, Willsford and Brown Windsor.

Brown Windsor, taking an extra stride before the fence, brought groans from the crowd as the normally sure-footed chaser capsized in spectacular style. Immediately behind him, Romany King did well to avoid a collision with the fallen horse, while Party Politics' gaping stride came in handy as he nimbly stepped over Brown Windsor.

Willsford and Golden Minstrel were jumping boldly together out in front as they raced down the back and, coming back onto the racecourse, they led Ghofar,

A giant of a horse, Party Politics gobbled up the ground to deny Romany King in 1992.

Hotplate, Forest Ranger and Party Politics, and with Rowlandsons Jewels the only one to depart at the Chair. Over thirty of the starting line-up set off for another circuit, with Cool Ground still in touch in the middle of the pack, but Seagram struggling badly towards the rear.

Starting to run a very big race was the outsider Hotplate, trained by Red Rum's handler Donald McCain, and at the seventeenth he was disputing the lead; behind him, the fancied pair of Docklands Express and Cool Ground began to make noticeable moves.

With a loose horse situated in the ditch, Aintree veteran Bonanza Boy exited at the nineteenth, but a large number of horses remained in the hunt as they approached Becher's for a second time. Hotplate was now the leader from Willsford, with Richard Guest making rapid progress on Romany King, while Golden Minstrel, Party Politics, Forest Ranger and Stay On Tracks were all in the leading group at the big fence. Golden Minstrel made a mistake as he stumbled on the landing side while Mister Ed and Cloney Grange crashed out further back, showing that the fence still possessed its uncanny ability to catch horses out.

Jumping Valentine's and beyond, an incredible number of horses were still holding on to some sort of hope, with eighteen runners within touching distance of the lead. With long-time front-runners Golden Minstrel and Willsford beginning to fade away a little, Romany King and Party Politics emerged from the chasing pack to take command.

Party Politics was travelling extremely smoothly and treating the fences more like hurdles with his giant frame. Both he and Romany King were starting to increase the pace; rounding the final turn they had broken clear of the chasing pack, led by Stay On Tracks, Docklands Express, Ghofar, Cool Ground, Hotplate and Old Applejack.

Over the remaining two fences, Llewellyn urged Party Politics into a relentless gallop and, jumping the obstacles economically, his huge stride simply devoured the ground once he was on the flat.

Romany King had not given up, however, and chasing the big horse frantically, his challenge reached its most threatening at the elbow. Unable to match the leader's march, he succumbed, to give Party Politics a most impressive victory by two-and-a-half lengths.

Laura's Beau plugged on steadily for third place, with Docklands Express – placed yet again in a major race – taking fourth. The top weight Twin Oaks, although never a serious threat, had stayed on admirably to beat a number of tired horses for fifth position. Not surprisingly, after having so many runners still in contention after the second Becher's, twenty-two horses managed to complete the course in a strangely incident free race.

The massive Party Politics had beaten them all, and gave the impression that, remaining healthy, he could return to Aintree and be a serious contender for a number of years, such was the manner of his victory. He was certainly young enough at just eight.

The victory was a crowning moment for trainer Nick Gaselee, and all the more creditable since the horse had suffered from wind troubles during his career and had undergone two operations to help eliminate the problem.

For Mr and Mrs Thompson, their late purchase had proved even more profitable than when they had bought Classified and Northern Bay before the 1986 National. On that occasion, Classified had finished third, but now they were the proud owners of the Grand National winner.

Another man feeling particularly proud, not to mention fortunate, was winning jockey Carl Llewellyn. Having failed to get round on Kumbi, and then unluckily on Smart Tar in his two previous rides in the race, Llewellyn had orchestrated a masterful ride and maximised the rangy stride of his winning mount over the last few fences. Of course, Llewellyn was only riding Party Politics because Andy Adams had fractured a leg at Doncaster six weeks before the race, and in the aftermath of the biggest win of his career, the twenty-six-year-old graciously made sure nobody forgot the unlucky situation of his stricken colleague.

HORSE/FATE		AGE/WEIGHT	JOCKEY	ODDS
1st	PARTY POLITICS	8.10-7	C. LLEWELLYN	14/1
2nd	ROMANY KING	8.10-3	R. GUEST	16/1
3rd	LAURA'S BEAU	8.10-0	C. O'DWYER	12/1
4th	DOCKLANDS EXPRESS	10.11-2	P. SCUDAMORE	15/2*
5th	Twin Oaks	12.11-7	N. Doughty	9/1
6th	Just So	9.10-2	S. Burrough	50/1
7th	Old Applejack	12.10-0	A. Orkney	35/1
8th	Over The Road	11.10-0	R. Supple	22/1
9th	Stay On Tracks	10.10-0	C. Grant	16/1
10th	Cool Ground	10.11-1	M. Lynch	10/1
11th	Ghofar	9.10-3	H. Davies	25/1
12th	Forest Ranger	10.10-0	D. Tegg	200/1
13th	What's The Crack	9.10-0	J. Osborne	20/1
14th	Rubika	9.10-2	P. Niven	28/1
15th	Golden Minstrel	13.10-0	E. Murphy	150/1
16th	Auntie Dot	11.10-7	M. Dwyer	12/1
17th	Roc De Prince	9.10-9	C. Swan	40/1
18th	Mighty Falcon	7.10-0	P. Holley	80/1
19th	Radical Lady	8.10-0	J. Callaghan	80/1
20th	Willsford	9.10-0	M. Bowlby	16/1
21st	Team Challenge	10.10-0	B. De Haan	100/1
22nd	Sirrah Jay	12.10-0	R.J. Beggan	100/1
Seagram - *Pulled Up*		12.11-4	N. Hawke	33/1
Bonanza Boy - *Unseated Rider*		11.10-11	S. Smith-Eccles	25/1
Brown Windsor - *Fell*		10.10-8	R. Dunwoody	8/1
Omerta - *Pulled Up*		12.10-4	L. Wyer	33/1
Huntworth - *Pulled Up*		12.10-0	M. Richards	66/1
Rawhide - *Unseated Rider*		8.10-0	K. O'Brien	50/1
Karakter Reference - *Pulled Up*		10.10-1	D. O'Sullivan	50/1
Rowlandsons Jewels - *Unseated Rider*		11.10-3	G. Bradley	60/1
Cloney Grange - *Fell*		13.10-0	D. O'Connor	100/1
New Halen - *Refused*		11.10-0	R. Bellamy	66/1
Hotplate - *Pulled Up*		9.10-5	G. McCourt	50/1
Mister Ed - *Fell*		9.10-0	D. Morris	100/1
Royal Battery - *Pulled Up*		9.10-0	R. Greene	80/1
Golden Fox - *Refused*		10.10-0	S. Earle	200/1
Stearsby - *Refused*		13.10-6	S. Mackey	250/1
Kittinger - *Refused*		11.10-0	I. Lawrence	200/1
Why So Hasty - *Pulled Up*		11.10-0	W. Worthington	250/1
Honeybeer Mead - *Unseated Rider*		10.10-0	N. Mann	100/1

1993
(RACE VOID)

Throughout its history, the Grand National at Aintree has been remembered for thrills and spills, high drama, excruciating tension, marvellous excitement and fabulous competitors. Above all, it is recognised as the world's greatest steeplechase. The 1993 version certainly provided moments of unforgettable action, giving the usual catalogue of magnificent horses and committed riders and probably more drama than any National that had been run before. However, without doubt, the 1993 Grand National turned out to be the most chaotic, laughable and depressing running of the event ever staged; it was a disaster.

The day of the race brought with it the usual unique excitement and optimism, as people all over the country scoured the morning newspapers for tips and advice on which horse to place their money on. The favourite was the previous year's hero, Party Politics, who had been pulled up on his first two runs of the season. Since his triumph the year before, the horse had been fitted with a special tube in his neck to aid his breathing, and the operation had paid dividends on his most recent start when he was victorious at Haydock Park. Again on board the strapping nine-year-old was Carl Llewellyn, who had won his race against time to be fit for the big day after suffering an injury at the Cheltenham Festival.

The horse Party Politics had beaten over the closing stages twelve months ago, Romany King, had long been an ante-post fancy for the big race. Now under the ownership of Mr Urs Schwarzenbach, a Swiss banker, but still trained by Toby Balding, the horse had been given the Grand National as his premier target for the season. Although he had not enjoyed a huge portion of success during a light build-up, the fact that he had performed so admirably on his National debut in 1992 resulted in him being a very popular selection on the day.

Sharing second place in the market on 15/2 with Romany King, was one of the most improved chasers in the land. Zeta's Lad had enjoyed a marvellous season, which had simply got better the longer it went on. Trained by John Upson, Zeta's Lad had won five races in a row, including the valuable Thyestes Chase at Gowran Park and the *Racing Post* Chase at Kempton Park. It was the latter victory which convinced Upson that Zeta's Lad should go for the National, where the horse had just 10st 4lb to carry. With the trainer full of confidence that this was to be his horse's year, Robbie Supple took the mount on the impressive ten-year-old.

Looking to train her second Grand National winner ten years after Corbiere, Jenny Pitman had a particularly strong team on this occasion. Most fancied of her three runners was Royal Athlete, who had finished an excellent third in the recent Cheltenham Gold Cup. Having won five chases as a novice, Royal Athlete had then missed a lot of the next two seasons with injuries, but his ability to stay long distances saw him heavily backed at 17/2. Garrison Savannah was back at Aintree, having been an absentee twelve months before, and his latest run had seen him finish seventh in the Gold Cup. Realising the horse had valuable previous experience of the big fences, Mark Pitman elected to partner the former Gold Cup winner rather than Royal Athlete. Least heralded of the Pitman team was the capable ten-

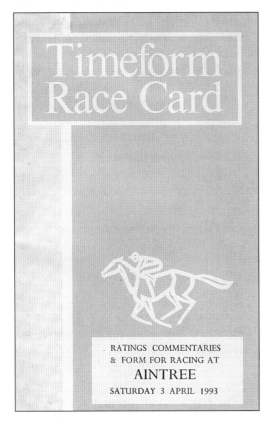

RATINGS COMMENTARIES
& FORM FOR RACING AT
AINTREE
SATURDAY 3 APRIL 1993

year-old Esha Ness. The horse had slumped to fifth place in the Kim Muir Chase at the Cheltenham Festival, after starting favourite. At Aintree, he would have the experienced John White, second in 1987 on The Tsarevich, to guide him round.

Captain Dibble, On The Other Hand, The Committee and Quirinus were all interesting challengers for the 1993 race. The inconsistent Captain Dibble had the ever-popular Peter Scudamore on board and had won the Scottish Grand National the previous season, while On The Other Hand was the latest challenger from the Gordon Richards yard. Although he did not carry quite the same stable optimism as previous recent runners Dark Ivy, Rinus and Twin Oaks, On The Other Hand had won the Grand Military Gold Cup at Sandown and had Aintree specialist Neale Doughty as his jockey. The Committee, trained by Homer Scott and fresh from an impressive display in the Kim Muir Chase at Cheltenham, was a strong Irish representative, while the previous year's Velka Pardubicka winner, Quirinus, lined up with Czechoslovakia's champion jockey Jaroslav Brecka in the saddle.

With Just So ruled out on the day due to unfavourable going, thirty-nine runners assembled at the start and were greeted by strong winds and driving rain. What happened next, regrettably, can only be described as a shambles.

As millions of people all over the world tuned in to watch the famous race, an already late start was delayed further when the usual suspects of protestors and demonstrators decided to make their presence felt in front of the first fence. Their exhibition, which was becoming all-too-frequent an occurrence before Grand Nationals, was pointed out to starter Keith Brown by concerned jockeys, and the increasingly frustrated horses were forced to turn away and wait some more.

With Chatam and Royle Speedmaster proving particularly quarrelsome, the fidgety runners were once more called into line. Eager to get them on their way, the starter raised the tape, but the feeble-looking device was clobbered by a number of runners, resulting in a false start. The flagman in front of the first fence, Ken Evans, successfully signalled to the charging runners, and they soon retreated for another try.

With the crowd becoming increasingly loud and irritated, the confusion at the start was mounting up. As the field got back into line, the stubbornness of some of the horses was beginning to reach crisis levels, as they, understandably, reacted to all the fuss and yelling.

Finally sent off again, the majority of the field got away successfully, but on the wide outside the slow-rising tape caught Richard Dunwoody around the neck, giving him no chance of continuing on Wont Be Gone Long, while eight others were also stopped in their tracks. Shouting frantically as thirty of the field hurtled unknowingly away in the distance, Keith Brown tried in vain to recall the runners again after another false start. With the flagman apparently missing in action, the field began a most surreal journey over the famous obstacles.

To a stunned silence, Sure Metal, Rowlandsons Jewels and Cahervillahow jumped the first in the lead, and mercifully there were no fallers until the grey Farm Week capsized at the fourth.

Flying Becher's, Donald McCain's runner Sure Metal led Romany King, Howe Street, Givus A Buck and Interim Lib and when they got to the Canal Turn, a chorus of disapproval echoed down from the spectators.

Royal Athlete was the next to fall at the tenth, and as Sure Metal and Howe Street led them back on to the racecourse, an eerie silence ghosted over the tannoy commentary.

Awaiting the field at the Chair were a number of traffic cones, randomly placed in front of the obstacle, while a flag-bearing official tried desperately to attract the attention of the runners and get them to pull up. No doubt utterly confused by what they were faced with, the field jumped the mighty fence and, as they carried on, the grandstand erupted with a vicious assault of booing.

It was only when they reached the start again, where nine of the runners still stood innocently watching the farce, that many who had completed one circuit saw their own trainers and colleagues waving at them to stop, and duly reacted by pulling up, including fancied horses Party Politics, Zeta's Lad, Captain Dibble and Garrison Savannah.

But for others at the head of affairs, how could they possibly give up their chance of winning a Grand National when they were not sure what was going on? Although a number of continuing jockeys looked round to see just how many of their fellow competitors were dropping out, they carried on their quest amidst deafening silence.

When disputing leaders Sure Metal and Howe Street plunged to the ground simultaneously at the twentieth, eight horses were left to endure an arduous battle over the remaining fences, and with Romany King and The Committee taking command as they jumped the flights down the back, they were reduced to seven when Interim Lib unseated his rider at the Canal Turn.

With the two leaders beginning to tire at the last fence, Esha Ness continued the steady progress he had been making to take the lead on the flat. Staying on strongly for John White, Esha Ness galloped to the line to faint applause, edging the hard-driven Cahervillahow. Romany King, The Committee, Givus A Buck, On The Other Hand and Laura's Beau followed them home, having successfully completed the most demanding of steeplechases for nothing.

Within seconds of finishing what he believed was his most glorious moment in the sport, John White was given the shattering news that the most confusing and weird of Nationals he had participated in was, in fact, to be declared void because of the false start. The heart-broken look on the face of the gallant White – as he realised his dreams had been crushed and the magnificent ride he had given the brave Esha Ness would be rendered meaningless – bore great testimony to the significance that the famous race has for its competitors. Fortunately, no horses were killed in the chaos, although Travel Over sustained a serious injury following the mishap at the start, while others had needlessly fallen over the course of two circuits.

It was originally suggested that the nine horses that did not jump a fence: Wont Be Gone Long, Chatam, Tarqogan's Best, Nos Na Gaoithe, Kildimo, Formula One, Roc De Prince, Royle Speedmaster and Latent Talent, be allowed their chance of victory in a nine-runner National, but after much discussion and a great deal of disapproval, the race was declared officially void with all bets to be refunded and no chance of a replacement race to be run.

The reactions of the jockeys and trainers included anger, frustration and sadness, with the Jockey Club receiving most of the blame and being branded unprofessional in their approach to the race. It was clear that if the Grand National was to reclaim its place as a great event in the sporting calendar, drastic and thorough changes would have to take place to ensure that what happened to the disastrous 1993 edition never occurred again.

The 'winner' Esha Ness (25), The Committee (centre) and Romany King were three of the seven who completed the course to no avail.

HORSE/FATE	AGE/WEIGHT	JOCKEY	ODDS
1st **ESHA NESS**	**10.10-0**	**J. WHITE**	**50/1**
2nd **CAHERVILLAHOW**	**9.10-11**	**C. SWAN**	**25/1**
3rd **ROMANY KING**	**9.10-7**	**A. MAGUIRE**	**15/2**
4th **THE COMMITTEE**	**10.10-0**	**N. WILLIAMSON**	**25/1**
5th Givus A Buck	10.10-0	P. Holley	16/1
6th On The Other Hand	10.10-3	N. Doughty	20/1
7th Laura's Beau	9.10-0	C. O'Dwyer	20/1
Quirinus - *Pulled Up*	11.11-10	J. Brecka	300/1
Garrison Savannah - *Pulled Up*	10.11-8	M. Pitman	10/1
Chatam - *Left*	9.11-10	J. Lower	28/1
Party Politics - *Pulled Up*	9.11-2	C. Llewellyn	7/1*
Captain Dibble - *Pulled Up*	8.10-8	P. Scudamore	9/1
Royal Athlete - *Fell*	10.10-4	B. De Haan	17/2
Zeta's Lad - *Pulled Up*	10.10-4	R. Supple	15/2
Joyful Noise - *Refused*	10.10-1	T. Jarvis	150/1
Roc De Prince - *Left*	10.10-6	G. McCourt	66/1
Riverside Boy - *Pulled Up*	10.10-0	M. Perrett	28/1
Bonanza Boy - *Refused*	12.10-0	S. McNeill	100/1
Sure Metal - *Fell*	10.10-0	S.J. O'Neill	50/1
The Gooser - *Fell*	10.10-0	K. O'Brien	50/1
Latent Talent - *Left*	9.10-2	J. Osborne	28/1
Rowlandsons Jewels - *Pulled Up*	12.10-0	D. Gallagher	50/1
Kildimo - *Left*	13.10-0	L. Wyer	40/1
New Mill House - *Pulled Up*	10.10-0	T. Horgan	66/1
Howe Street - *Fell*	10.10-0	A. Orkney	66/1
David's Duky - *Pulled Up*	11.10-0	M. Brennan	100/1
Wont Be Gone Long - *Left*	11.10-1	R. Dunwoody	16/1
Travel Over - *Pulled Up*	12.10-2	Mr M. Armytage	100/1
Nos Na Gaoithe - *Left*	10.10-2	R. Garritty	66/1
Stay On Tracks - *Pulled Up*	11.10-0	K. Johnson	50/1
Paco's Boy - *Fell*	8.10-0	M. Foster	100/1
Formula One - *Left*	11.10-0	Judy Davies	200/1
Senator Snugfit - *Fell*	8.10-0	Peter Hobbs	200/1
Mister Ed - *Pulled Up*	10.10-0	D. Morris	25/1
Tarqogans Best - Left	13.10-0	B. Clifford	500/1
Farm Week - *Fell*	11.10-1	S. Hodgson	200/1
Interim Lib - *Unseated Rider*	10.10-4	Mr J. Bradburne	200/1
Direct - *Pulled Up*	10.10-3	P. Niven	100/1
Royle Speedmaster - *Left*	9.10-5	Mr J. Durkan	200/1

1994
MIINNEHOMA

The changes made at Aintree to eradicate the problems that had ruined the previous year's race were both sensible and efficient. Over £1 million had been spent on overall security, with perimeter fences erected to stop people rushing onto the course to demonstrate. The much maligned, hand-operated starting tape was replaced by a considerably faster electronic gate, which was raised with a simple push of a button. To eliminate unnecessary confusion for the starter, nobody was allowed within fifty yards of his rostrum, while three new flagmen, all former jockeys, were positioned further down the course to provide added assistance.

In one of the most competitive fields for a number of years, the brilliant recent Cheltenham Gold Cup winner The Fellow provided an extra-special dose of class to the 1994 Grand National. Trained in France by the masterful Francois Doumen, The Fellow was a superb jumper and possessed both stamina and courage. In addition to the Gold Cup, the horse was a former winner of the Grand Steeplechase de Paris and had also captured a pair of King George VI Chases at Kempton Park. Although the barrage of wet weather that occurred throughout the week had threatened his participation at one point, the horse, owned by Marquesa de Moratalla and ridden by Polish jockey Adam Kondrat, was allowed to take his chance in the greatest race of them all.

Having won nine hunter-chases in a row, including the Aintree Foxhunter's in the previous campaign, Double Silk was also considered a premier candidate for National glory. Owned and trained by Mr Reg Wilkins, the horse had taken all before him in his division and had a bold-jumping, front-running style that was ideally suited to Aintree. Double Silk had never fallen in his career, and ridden by amateur Ron Treloggen, he took his place among seasoned handicappers with a large amount of support.

Eclipsing both The Fellow and Double Silk in the betting, however, was the tough stayer Moorcroft Boy. Trained by David Nicholson, the horse was an ex-hunter-chaser who revelled in the testing conditions that lay ahead in the National, and he had taken a pair of decent chases at Cheltenham and Warwick in January. Ridden by Adrian Maguire, the consistent chaser wound up starting as 5/1 favourite for the big race.

The dark horse for the 1994 race was the eight-year-old Master Oats. Having missed the entire previous season with leg trouble, the horse had won four of his five races during the season and last time out had demolished the favourite Moorcroft Boy in the Greenhalls Gold Cup to leap into National consideration. Trained by Kim Bailey, already a winner with Mr Frisk in 1990, Master Oats was another horse that appreciated softer conditions, and with Norman Williamson riding, the horse was backed at 9/1.

If Master Oats had only recently emerged as a chaser of genuine quality, then Miinnehoma was one that was trying to re-ignite a once promising career. One of five runners on this occasion for Martin Pipe, Miinnehoma had won the Royal & Sun Alliance Chase at the Cheltenham Festival during his novice season, but since then a combination of injury and poor form had seen his progression stunted. The horse had returned from a long lay-off to win at Newbury earlier in the season and that was followed by an encouraging effort in the Cheltenham Gold Cup. With the expertise of Richard Dunwoody to guide him round, and the rain falling in his favour, Miinnehoma was another to command frequent support in the betting market.

With a plethora of highly talented chasers in the field, horses that attracted considerable attention were Young Hustler, Just So and Fiddlers Pike. Young Hustler, an extremely game warrior, was trying to become the first seven-year-old to win since Bogskar in 1940 and had recently finished third in the Cheltenham Gold Cup, while Just So (often referred to as 'Just Slow') was a dour stayer who loved the mud and had won the John Hughes Grand National Trial at Chepstow in February in heavy going. Fiddlers Pike, a steady jumping thirteen-year-old, was partnered by his fifty-one-year-old owner and trainer, Mrs Rosemary Henderson, who had to receive special permission from the Jockey Club to take part.

With relentless heavy rain on the Friday causing some doubts as to whether the National could take place at all, it took a morning inspection on the day of the race before the go-ahead was given. Clearly, the race was going to be a severe test of stamina, with the ground extremely heavy. Even so, the runners – reduced from the thirty-nine declared to thirty-six when Bishops Hall, Windy Ways and Rifle Range withdrew in the morning – were bathed in sunshine as the new starting gate went up as smoothly as planned to send them on their way.

Immediately, Double Silk set about his front-running tactics and, together with Young Hustler in the centre of the track, they led at the first from Garrison Savannah on the inside. In behind them, Henry Mann, Fourth Of July and the fancied Elfast crashed down on the mushy ground, while Ushers Island and Aintree veteran Romany King soon followed at the third and fourth fences.

Approaching Becher's Brook, it was noticeable that the horses were travelling much slower than normal, and even at this early stage, some were starting to trail dramatically towards the back. It was Double Silk and Riverside Boy that led Young Hustler and Garrison Savannah at the famous fence, which brought about the downfall of New Mill House and It's A Cracker.

The leading quartet over Becher's remained in position and, with Double Silk in particular jumping like a stag, they continued their march over Valentine's Brook and beyond. At the eleventh, however, Young Hustler was the victim of an unlucky incident, as a loose horse crashed to the ground directly in front of him, giving David Bridgwater's mount no chance as he landed over the fence.

Coming back onto the racecourse, Double Silk had settled into a steady rhythm and was going really well. However, as he met the usually innocuous thirteenth fence, a loose horse directly in front of him stumbled, possibly putting the fancied runner off his stride. Brushing through the top of the obstacle, Double Silk came down to suffer his first ever fall, while behind him chaos broke out as Master Oats also fell when moving up nicely on the outside – both Topsham Bay and Mighty Falcon were put out of the race amidst the confusion. With Mr Boston also falling towards the back, the entire picture of the race had changed at one fence.

More drama followed at the Chair as Black Humour, who had been progressing quietly behind the leaders, landed on top of the fence and was cannoned into by the rider-less Double Silk, both horses then plummeting to the ground.

All this had left a vastly strung-out field to slog round for another circuit, and with both the leaders, Garrison Savannah and Riverside Boy, refusing at the seventeenth and eighteenth respectively, a group of just eleven were left standing on the run to Becher's for a second time.

The Irish runner Ebony Jane and Miinnehoma had taken up the running and they jumped the fence clear. Tracking the pair, The Fellow made a mistake which almost eliminated him from the race. Two fences later though, he was definitely out as he plunged to the floor at the Canal Turn, then collided dangerously with Mister Ed as he tried to get to his feet, knocking that rival out of the contest.

With the considerable threat of the Gold Cup winner now out of the way, a band of four horses, Ebony Jane, Miinnehoma, Just So and Moorcroft Boy found themselves clear of the chasing Into The Red as they jumped the final fences down the back before returning onto the racecourse.

As the brave horses reached the end of their gruelling marathon, it was Moorcroft Boy that landed in front over the last fence and a thunderous roar erupted from favourite-backers as Adrian Maguire urged his mount into one final, exhausting burst up the rain-soaked finish.

However, having been coolly ridden by Richard Dunwoody, Miinnehoma had craftily reserved some energy for the finale, and taking over at the elbow, he swept past the favourite with mud spraying in all directions. Suddenly, just as it seemed as if Miinnehoma would coast home, the rangy, imposing dark frame of Just So and jockey Simon Burrough loomed up on the outside to threaten the leader's position, and relishing the treacherous conditions, Just So rapidly began to eat away at the gap between the two horses.

Showing fantastically courageous fighting spirit, Miinnehoma mustered one last surge and was able to hold Just So at bay in a thrilling conclusion, rounded off by a punch of delight from the triumphant Dunwoody. The first two home had shown the utmost bravery in battling to the end after an almighty slog through extremely testing National conditions, as had Moorcroft Boy back in third and Ebony Jane in fourth. Mrs Henderson managed to complete the course in a highly creditable fifth place, with Roc De Prince the only other survivor.

Not surprisingly, the winning time was the slowest since 1955 but, thankfully, all the horses returned home safely.

The win capped Richard Dunwoody's standing as one of the finest jockeys of the modern era, and arrived eight years after his initial National win on West Tip. With Miinnehoma, he had succeeded on a 'forgotten' horse – owned by comedian Freddie Starr – that had finally fulfilled the potential of his early career.

Martin Pipe had at last won the Grand National, having been one of the leading trainers for a number of years. In general, after such a disappointing occasion in 1993,

One of the best trainers of all-time, Martin Pipe, gained his first Grand National courtesy of the mud-loving Miinnehoma.

the 1994 renewal successfully restored the National to its proud and lofty position in the world of sport.

HORSE/FATE	AGE/WEIGHT	JOCKEY	ODDS
1st **MIINNEHOMA**	**11.10-8**	**R. DUNWOODY**	**16/1**
2nd **JUST SO**	**11.10-3**	**S. BURROUGH**	**20/1**
3rd **MOORCROFT BOY**	**9.10-0**	**A. MAGUIRE**	**5/1***
4th **EBONY JANE**	**9.10-1**	**L. CUSACK**	**25/1**
5th Fiddlers Pike	13.10-0	Mrs R. Henderson	100/1
6th Roc De Prince	11.10-0	J. Lower	100/1
Quirinus - *Unseated Rider*	12.11-10	J. Brecka	250/1
Run For Free - *Refused*	10.11-7	M. Perrett	25/1
The Fellow - *Fell*	9.11-4	A. Kondrat	9/1
Zeta's Lad - *Fell*	11.10-13	R. Supple	16/1
Young Hustler - *Brought Down*	7.10-12	D. Bridgwater	16/1
Black Humour - *Fell*	10.10-12	G. Bradley	33/1
Topsham Bay - *Unseated Rider*	11.10-11	J. Frost	25/1
Double Silk - *Fell*	10.10-4	Mr R. Treloggen	6/1
Garrison Savannah - *Refused*	11.10-3	J. Osborne	25/1
Romany King - *Fell*	10.10-1	R. Guest	22/1
Riverside Boy - *Refused*	11.10-0	M. Richards	33/1
Rust Never Sleeps - *Fell*	10.10-0	P. Carberry	66/1
Henry Mann - *Fell*	11.10-0	C. Swan	50/1
Mr Boston - *Fell*	9.10-2	P. Niven	16/1
Master Oats - *Fell*	8.10-0	N. Williamson	9/1
Gay Ruffian - *Fell*	8.10-0	R. Farrant	150/1
Ushers Island - *Unseated Rider*	8.10-0	A. Dobbin	66/1
Elfast - *Fell*	11.10-4	G. McCourt	18/1
Into The Red - *Unseated Rider*	10.10-0	J. White	25/1
Mister Ed - *Brought Down*	11.10-0	D. Morris	50/1
Captain Brandy - *Unseated Rider*	9.10-0	K. O'Brien	50/1
Southern Minstrel - *Pulled Up*	11.10-1	M. Dwyer	50/1
Laura's Beau - *Fell*	10.10-0	B. Sheridan	40/1
Fourth Of July - *Fell*	10.10-0	J.P. Banahan	50/1
New Mill House - *Fell*	11.10-0	T. Horgan	150/1
It's A Cracker - *Fell*	10.10-0	C. O'Dwyer	33/1
Paco's Boy - *Pulled Up*	9.10-0	M. Foster	200/1
He Who Dares Wins - *Pulled Up*	11.10-0	C. Grant	66/1
Channels Gate - *Refused*	10.10-0	T. Jenks	100/1
Mighty Falcon - *Brought Down*	9.10-0	P. Holley	250/1

1995
ROYAL ATHLETE

Continuing the sequence set by Garrison Savannah, Cool Ground and The Fellow in the early 1990s, the 1995 Grand National was to be graced by the latest Cheltenham Gold Cup winner. On this occasion, the horse was the much improved and deeply impressive Master Oats. Having illustrated his potential to many before falling in the 1994 National, Master Oats had remained unbeaten in his four chases during the season, including his comfortable, strong-galloping success at Cheltenham in soft conditions. Despite lingering doubts over both his jumping ability – because of a number of mistakes made during his Gold Cup win – and the prospect of him handling fast-drying ground at Aintree, trainer Kim Bailey displayed supreme confidence in his charge, and the horse started a rock-solid 5/1 favourite after being given the all-clear to run on the morning of the race.

Very much a popular horse with the public, Young Hustler had been an unlucky casualty in the previous year's event. With bravery and consistency two of his traits, the horse trained by Nigel Twiston-Davies had strung together a strong series of results, and his latest start had seen him finish fifth in the Cheltenham Gold Cup on unfavourably soft ground. With the going considerably more to his liking at Aintree, Young Hustler was highly fancied to run a very big race.

In the days leading up to the National, one horse that became increasingly popular in the betting market was the relatively unexposed chestnut Country Member. Having been injured the previous season, the horse had advertised his National chances with a fine win in the Grand Military Gold Cup at Sandown Park on his latest outing, and the good ground at Aintree was deemed ideal for him. With Luke Harvey taking the ride, Country Member was well supported at 11/1 for glory.

One horse whose abundance of stamina almost guaranteed a bold showing was the nine-year-old mare Dubacilla. The horse was a half-sister to Just So, who had run so gamely to finish second in the previous National, and like Just So, Dubacilla's style was to come from off the pace and try to strike late on. This trend had continued in the recent Cheltenham Gold Cup where, making up tremendous late ground, Dubacilla failed only to reel in the runaway winner Master Oats. With the Gold Cup winner now the only one in front of her in the betting, Dubacilla started next in the list at 9/1.

Recent National winners Miinnehoma and Party Politics again returned to Aintree in a bid for further success. After winning his opening race of the season, Miinnehoma went on to finish third in the Gold Cup, but at Aintree, he had 9lb more to carry than in his 1994 victory, while the ground conditions were much faster than the mud-covered turf that he triumphed on the previous year. Having missed the 1994 race through injury, Party Politics was attempting to rekindle his past form. Mark Dwyer's mount had generally proved below par during the season, and on his last run before the National, the eleven-year-old was disappointingly pulled up.

With six runners to represent her, Jenny Pitman saddled the highest number of horses of any trainer in the National. The most fancied of the six at 12/1 was fast ground specialist

Lusty Light, who had recently won at Wincanton, while the stable's number one jockey, Warren Marston, elected to ride Garrison Savannah, due to the former Gold Cup hero's previous exploits over the fearsome fences. After his void victory in 1993, Esha Ness was back as a twelve-year-old to try and win a National for real with John White aboard, while Superior Finish and outsider Do Be Brief would be having their first tastes of the National. Completing the team was another twelve-year-old, Royal Athlete. Well fancied when falling in the void race, the horse had a history of leg troubles, and four days before the Cheltenham Gold Cup, he picked up another knock that ruled him out of that contest. With mediocre recent form to his name, Royal Athlete and Aintree first-timer Jason Titley were generally unconsidered and were sent off at 40/1.

As the sun beamed down on the Aintree turf, giving the course a radiant appearance, the smaller-than-normal field of thirty-five were unleashed to a first-time start, again proving the excellence of the new system.

They were going a cracking pace on the good ground as Topsham Bay and Over The Deel led the charge to the first fence. As the leaders sailed over safely, there was mayhem in behind as seven horses were put out of the race. Country Member's big white face hit the floor as he came down together with Lusty Light, The Committee, Tinryland and Bishops Hall, while Errant Knight unseated his rider and the unlucky Jumbeau was brought down. No sooner had the dust settled at the first fence, when more shocks took place, as Young

Trainer Kim Bailey with his much-fancied 1995 prospect Master Oats.

Hustler, disputing the lead on the inside, clipped the third fence extremely hard and sent Carl Llewellyn flying from the saddle, much to the disappointment of the crowd. Zeta's Lad and General Pershing also made exits from the contest at the big ditch, with the departure of the former leaving jockey Graham Bradley unconscious.

As they faced up to Becher's Brook for the first time, two of the Pitman team, Superior Finish and Do Be Brief, held the lead from fast-ground loving Topsham Bay, a dual Whitbread Gold Cup winner, with Cheltenham hero Master Oats being given plenty of daylight by Norman Williamson on the wide outside. As the leaders flew over the famous fence, Miinnehoma was struggling badly at the rear, having made a mistake at the first flight, and he was now a good 100 yards from the pacesetters.

The shrinking field was reduced by one more as leader Superior Finish stumbled badly after jumping the tenth, unseating Peter Niven in the process, while Chatam and Esha Ness came to grief two fences later. As the depleted group came back onto the racecourse, it was Do Be Brief that held the advantage. Due to the large number of early casualties, many loose horses surrounded the runners at the Chair, but unlike Nationals past, they thankfully failed to cause any trouble as the field rose at the magnificent obstacle; going out for another circuit, Do Be Brief led Crystal Spirit, Camelot Knight, Garrison Savannah, Ebony Jane, Master Oats and Royal Athlete as the race began to intensify.

Moving quietly forward on the inside, Jason Titley was enjoying a dream ride on Royal Athlete, who was showing no ill-effects from his fall over the fences two years before, and leaving the tumbling Do Be Brief and Camelot Knight behind, as well as the grey outsider Desert Lord, Royal Athlete led as Becher's lay in wait. Master Oats was beginning to make his challenge on the outside, having stayed out of trouble for a circuit, while 100/1 shot Over The Deel was running the race of his life in the middle of the track as the trio took the big fence.

Down the back, Royal Athlete and Master Oats indulged in a fascinating duel for the lead, with both jumping exceptionally well and opening up a gap from the chasing pack. But it was the lighter-weighted Royal Athlete that was travelling the easier of the two, and as they crossed the Melling Road for the final time, he had the Gold Cup winner under pressure.

Coming to the second last, old adversaries Party Politics and Romany King had rolled up to join the leaders, and an exciting, multi-horse finish looked in prospect. Still jumping like a buck, Royal Athlete flew over the final flight from Master Oats and Party Politics and set off towards the elbow.

The giant 1992 winner was gaining ground with every stride, and cruised past the weakening Master Oats to challenge the leader. However, given expert encouragement from Titley, Royal Athlete was not to be denied in these late stages, and the manner in which he accelerated clear to the line showed him to be a truly fine horse.

Saluting the win, Titley drove Royal Athlete over the finishing line with Party Politics his closest pursuer. Over The Deel carried Mr Chris Bonner home in third place in a dream first ride for the amateur, with Dubacilla – who typically had made up a lot of ground late on – flying home for fourth, in front of a close-finishing Into The Red and Romany King. A tired Master Oats came in a valiant seventh. The mare Dubacilla was graciously retired after the race, having made a pleasing exit from her racing career.

Royal Athlete had emerged as a superb winner of the race, and had given a tantalising insight into what he might have achieved in his career had it not been for injuries. Dominating on the second circuit, he had got the better of a fine battle with Gold Cup winner Master Oats before destroying a host of good horses with a clinical finishing burst. The win was a most welcome one for Jason Titley, who had ridden only seven winners during the season, and the Irishman had orchestrated a perfect ride down the inside on Royal Athlete.

Jenny Pitman's reputation as the first lady of Aintree was now even more enhanced following her second National winner, and much credit (rightfully) fell on her shoulders after the admirable way she had produced the horse she called 'Alfie' to capture the National, despite a string of injury blows. However, Mrs Pitman had the horse's owners, Mr Garry and Mrs Libby Johnson, to thank on this occasion after they requested that the horse run at Aintree in preference to the Scottish Grand National.

Success for all concerned was richly deserved and, once more, the Grand National had produced a race of tremendous quality with a fairytale result.

The Jenny Pitman team with 40/1 winner Royal Athlete.

HORSE/FATE	AGE/WEIGHT	JOCKEY	ODDS
1st **ROYAL ATHLETE**	**12.10-6**	**J. TITLEY**	**40/1**
2nd **PARTY POLITICS**	**11.10-2**	**M. DWYER**	**16/1**
3rd **OVER THE DEEL**	**9.10-0**	**MR C. BONNER**	**100/1**
4th **DUBACILLA**	**9.11-0**	**D. GALLAGHER**	**9/1**
5th Into The Red	11.10-0	R. Guest	20/1
6th Romany King	11.10-0	Mr M. Armytage	40/1
7th Master Oats	9.11-10	N. Williamson	5/1*
8th Riverside Boy	12.10-0	C. Swan	40/1
9th Garrison Savannah	12.10-0	W. Marston	16/1
10th Topsham Bay	12.10-0	P. Hide	20/1
11th Cool Ground	13.10-0	P. Holley	50/1
12th Ebony Jane	10.10-0	A. Maguire	20/1
13th Gold Cap	10.10-6	G. McCourt	50/1
14th Crystal Spirit	8.10-4	J. Osborne	12/1
15th For William	9.10-0	C. O'Dwyer	100/1
Miinnehoma - *Pulled Up*	12.11-4	R. Dunwoody	11/1
Young Hustler - *Unseated Rider*	8.11-2	C. Llewellyn	10/1
Chatam - *Fell*	11.10-6	A.P. McCoy	25/1
Zeta's Lad - *Unseated Rider*	12.10-3	G. Bradley	50/1
Lusty Light - *Fell*	9.10-2	R. Farrant	12/1
Nuaffe - *Fell*	10.10-0	S. O'Donovan	20/1
General Pershing - *Fell*	9.10-0	D. Bridgwater	20/1
Country Member - *Fell*	10.10-0	L. Harvey	11/1
Bishops Hall - *Fell*	9.10-0	C. Maude	66/1
Dakyns Boy - *Unseated Rider*	10.10-0	T. Jenks	50/1
Errant Knight - *Unseated Rider*	11.10-0	M. Perrett	75/1
Tinryland - *Fell*	11.10-2	M. Fitzgerald	50/1
Superior Finish - *Unseated Rider*	9.10-3	P. Niven	33/1
The Committee - *Fell*	12.10-0	T. Tanaka	75/1
Esha Ness - *Fell*	12.10-0	J. White	50/1
Desert Lord - *Fell*	9.10-0	F. Woods	100/1
Jumbeau - *Brought Down*	10.10-0	S. McNeill	100/1
Do Be Brief - *Fell*	10.10-0	B. Powell	66/1
Camelot Knight - *Fell*	9.10-2	Mr M. Rimell	66/1
It's A Snip - *Unseated Rider*	10.10-0	J.R. Kavanagh	200/1

1996
ROUGH QUEST

The most celebrated Grand National winner of all-time, Red Rum, three times a magnificent victor during the 1970s, passed away before the 1996 Grand National. Fittingly, the great warrior was laid to rest near the winning post at Aintree, as the racecourse honoured the horse that had captured the hearts and imaginations of sporting fans everywhere during his illustrious National career.

Whether there was another horse capable of performing up to the great legend's standards among the 1996 field remained to be seen, but there was certainly a collection of worthy challengers in a worryingly small field of twenty-seven.

The horse that was to claim the focus more than any of his competitors was the hugely talented ten-year-old Rough Quest. Having finished second to the electric Irish youngster Imperial Call in the recent Cheltenham Gold Cup, Rough Quest would have only sixteen days before Aintree to recover from his brave exploits – originally, his trainer, Terry Casey, had not intended to run the horse in the National, but with Rough Quest performing incredibly well, Casey eventually elected to run his star chaser, who had also been second in the season's Hennessy Gold Cup. Having his second ride in the race after falling at the first on Tinryland the previous year, Mick Fitzgerald was the man in the saddle, and although Rough Quest had been listed at much lower odds during the week leading up to the National, the drying ground saw him go off as the 7/1 favourite.

Having failed to get round in the previous two Grand Nationals, Young Hustler had demonstrated just what he was capable of over the big fences by taking the Becher Chase in November. Young Hustler had also run well in the Cheltenham Gold Cup and now ground conditions were turning in his favour at Aintree, with good going awaiting the runners. Despite the burden of top weight, the popular nine-year-old started joint second in the betting at 8/1.

It had been more than twenty years since an Irish runner had been victorious in the National, but on this occasion three horses in particular posed serious threats to breaking the losing streak. The horses were Life Of A Lord, Son Of War and Wylde Hide. The imposing Life Of A Lord was a first Grand National runner for the brilliant young trainer Aiden O'Brien and the horse had won four races earlier in the season, while he was also a lover of the good ground present for the 1996 race. The grey Son Of War was a very popular selection on the day and was a previous winner of the Irish Grand National, while his trainer, Peter McCreery, firmly believed his horse could win. Although he preferred a softer surface, Wylde Hide came into the race in cracking form having won his last two races, including the Thyestes Chase in January, and was very much the dark horse of the National field, starting at 12/1 with Francis Woods on board.

In a Grand National lacking quality in depth, other notable contenders included Superior Finish, Deep Bramble and Encore Un Peu. One of only two Jenny Pitman runners on this occasion, Superior Finish had appeared to relish the awesome fences in 1995 before unseating his jockey at the tenth fence. Now, after a consistent season, he was among the favourites and had Aintree expert Richard Dunwoody to guide him round. Deep Bramble had been a leading contender for the previous year's National, but had been forced to miss the race after pulling muscles in the Gold Cup the month before. His entire season had been geared around finally turning out in the National, and after a warm-up race at Haydock Park, the thorough stayer met his goal. The problem for Deep Bramble was that the ground had turned faster than was ideal for him, but with fast-rising star Tony McCoy on board, Paul Nicholl's charge was sent off at 12/1. The shortest priced of Martin Pipe's three runners was the former French-trained gelding Encore Un Peu, and after a recent second in the Kim Muir Chase at the Cheltenham Festival, David Bridgwater's mount was quietly fancied at 14/1.

With the smallest field since the 1970 race being called in without delay, new starter Gerry Scott – who had ridden Merryman II to victory in 1960 – soon had them running to a roar of excitement in the basking sunshine.

The fast-breaking Captain Dibble was swiftly joined up front by Young Hustler and Superior Finish as they met the first fence. Over-jumping, Bavard Dieu gave the previous year's winning jockey Jason Titley a painful fall, while Bishops Hall went at the opening obstacle for the second year on the trot. Sure Metal and Three Brownies, a pair of rank outsiders, had quickly jumped through to take up the running, and as they set about forcing a searching gallop, the usually safe-jumping Party Politics shocked the watching crowd with an uncharacteristic tumble towards the rear.

Joined by Sir Peter Lely and Greenhill Raffles at the head of affairs, the leaders swept over Becher's Brook in glorious style and, most unusually, there was not a single casualty at the mighty fence and the race progressed with nearly all the starters still in the hunt as the action returned onto the racecourse. Sadly, before the thirteenth fence, the first tragedy since the 1991 race struck, as the twelve-year-old Rust Never Sleeps fractured a shoulder, which resulted in the brave horse later having to be put down.

Like Becher's, the Chair offered little anxiety to the well-bunched field, who were jumping particularly fluidly, and as they ventured out for a second circuit, a hotly-contested race was led by Three Brownies, with Sure Metal, Young Hustler, Over The Deel, Sir Peter Lely and Greenhill Raffles all in close attendance.

On the march down to Becher's for a second time, many of the fancied horses began to assert themselves on proceedings. Young Hustler hit the front, while Life Of A Lord and Rough Quest moved up smoothly on the outside. Deep Bramble too was not far behind, and although he was down on his nose as they flew across the Brook, the horse, like many others, remained in contention as they raced on.

The Canal Turn was the undoing of a large chunk of the Irish raid, as first Son Of War and then Wylde Hide unseated their riders at the sharp, ninety-degree turn, just as it looked like they were mounting serious challenges.

Young Hustler continued to jump from fence to fence in the lead, but Three Brownies was running the race of his life with stylish Irishman Paul Carberry on board; together with Sir Peter Lely and the rapidly improving Encore Un Peu, they steamed

The impressive Rough Quest survived a stewards' enquiry to win the 1996 edition.

over the back fences and across the Melling Road for the final time. As the unfortunate Deep Bramble broke down badly on the turn for home, the real danger to the leaders was obvious, as the nose-banded favourite Rough Quest cruised up on the outside. With Three Brownies throwing away his chance with a mistake two out, Sir Peter Lely outpaced, and Young Hustler severely burdened with top weight, it came down to a battle between Encore Un Peu and Rough Quest as they took the last fence.

The blazing chestnut Encore Un Peu was sent sprinting off towards the elbow by an eager Bridgwater, but Fitzgerald was merely biding his time on the favourite. At the elbow, Rough Quest was finally unleashed and, showing considerable quality, he accelerated past his rival and battled strongly up the straight. Although he veered across Encore Un Peu, it did not affect the final outcome, and Rough Quest crossed the line a thoroughly deserving winner.

The connections of Rough Quest had to endure a nerve-racking fifteen minutes as the expected Steward's enquiry was resolved, but when it fell correctly in their favour, the joy for all was unmistakable. The favourite had clinically justified his market position with a faultless round of jumping under a masterfully patient ride by Mick Fitzgerald.

Staying on in the later stages, Superior Finish followed home Encore Un Peu, with Sir Peter Lely a valiant fourth. The top-weight Young Hustler had run his heart out in fifth, while Three Brownies had given the fancied horses an extreme scare until finally fading after the second last.

Rough Quest, owned by Mr Andrew Wates, had given Terry Casey a memorable training victory. The horse had been plagued by a condition affecting his muscle enzymes and, understandably, had required a great deal of care and attention from his trainer. Casey could now look forward to an ambitious assault on the major races the following season, with the King George, Cheltenham Gold Cup and another crack at the National all on the agenda for the marvellous Aintree winner.

In the aftermath of his greatest riding success, jockey Mick Fitzgerald was left to summarise in most graphic terms the glorious manner in which Rough Quest had captured the Grand National. When pointing out that he had not enjoyed twelve minutes so much for a long time, Fitzgerald added that sex would be an anti-climax after his dream venture on the National winner!

Trainer Terry Casey with Rough Quest.

HORSE/FATE	AGE/WEIGHT	JOCKEY	ODDS
1st ROUGH QUEST	10.10-7	M.A. FITZGERALD	7/1*
2nd ENCORE UN PEU	9.10-0	D. BRIDGWATER	14/1
3rd SUPERIOR FINISH	10.10-3	R. DUNWOODY	9/1
4th SIR PETER LELY	9.10-0	MR.C. BONNER	33/1
5th Young Hustler	9.11-7	C. Maude	8/1
6th Three Brownies	9.10-0	P. Carberry	100/1
7th Life Of A Lord	10.11-6	C. Swan	10/1
8th Antonin	8.10-0	J. Burke	28/1
9th Over The Deel	10.10-0	Mr T. McCarthy	33/1
10th Vicompt De Valmont	11.10-1	P. Hide	22/1
11th Captain Dibble	11.10-0	T. Jenks	40/1
12th Riverside Boy	13.10-0	D. Walsh	66/1
13th Over The Stream	10.10-0	A. Thornton	50/1
14th Greenhill Raffles	10.10-0	M. Foster	100/1
15th Into The Red	12.10-0	R. Guest	33/1
16th Lusty Light	10.10-11	W. Marston	14/1
17th Sure Metal	13.10-1	D. McCain	200/1
Deep Bramble - *Pulled Up*	9.11-5	A.P .McCoy	12/1
Son Of War - *Unseated Rider*	9.11-0	C. O'Dwyer	8/1
Party Politics - *Fell*	12.10-11	C. Llewellyn	10/1
Chatam - *Pulled Up*	12.10-3	J. Lower	40/1
Rust Never Sleeps - *Pulled Up*	12.10-0	T. Horgan	20/1
Bishops Hall - *Unseated Rider*	10.10-1	Mr M. Armytage	22/1
Wylde Hide - *Unseated Rider*	9.10-0	F. Woods	12/1
Bavard Dieu - *Unseated Rider*	8.10-1	J.F. Titley	50/1
Brackenfield - *Unseated Rider*	10.10-0	Guy Lewis	100/1
Far Senior - *Pulled Up*	10.10-0	T. Eley	150/1

1997
LORD GYLLENE

The 1997 Grand National marked the 150th anniversary of the world's most famous steeple-chase. The celebrated event had never been in such a strong position, possessing solid and generous sponsorship, fantastic organisation, and a less intimidating nature after the successful modification of the fences. But the 1997 edition experienced something that no other race in National history, not even the ill-fated void race of 1993, could relate to.

A pleasant rise in numbers occurred after the poor turn-out of twenty-seven in 1996, with thirty-eight ready to go to post on this occasion. An intriguing mixture of high-class handi-cappers, legitimate Irish challengers, complete no-hopers and a former Cheltenham Gold Cup winner made for a Grand National with a variety of flavours. With horses being saddled shortly before the big race and with some already walking round the paddock, the excite-ment, as usual, was starting to grow to meteoric proportions. To say what happened next was a let-down was a severe understatement. Not only was it that, but it also illustrated the extremities of cowardice and spite that some people will demonstrate to instil fear and panic in fellow human beings, while at the same time ruining one of the most loved spec-tacles in the sporting calendar.

About an hour before the start time, a pair of coded telephone messages, threatening that bombs had been placed on the racecourse, were received by Merseyside police. Naturally, with the severity and extreme danger of these warnings, the only feasible action was taken. The stands were evacuated and, as the giant screen facing the grandstand displayed, all persons in all areas were requested to leave immediately. Within an hour, the stands and surrounding areas were desolate, as the bomb squad set about their task of securing the area. Due to the worrying nature of the incident and the sheer disruption caused to the course and some of the fences, the race was forced into postponement, with thousands of people left stranded in the city of Liverpool without belongings that had had to be left behind in their hasty exits. There were many heroes that weekend – not least the brave stable lads who defiantly refused to leave the stranded horses, and the generous people of Merseyside who rallied round to assist the wandering masses.

It was a testament to the courage of Aintree, horseracing and the British public as a whole that at 5.00 p.m. two days later, the race was finally run, sending the most emphatic message to terrorists that the 'show must go on'. There was no charge for admittance, and around 20,000 people turned up, many of them youngsters. Although no cars were allowed on the course and everyone was thoroughly searched on admission, the atmosphere the crowd created was magnificent. Understandably, some of the intended runners on Saturday had become excessively disturbed by what had happened, and two of them, Belmont King and Over The Stream, were withdrawn from the rescheduled race. Of the thirty-six that remained, the favourite on the day was the John O'Shea-trained eight-year-old Go Ballistic, who had won the Betterware Cup at Ascot during the season. However, his most notable run had come in the recent Cheltenham Gold Cup when, totally unconsidered, he stayed on strongly at the end to finish fourth to the rangy chestnut Mr Mulligan. As ever, the Gold

Cup was used as a first-rate indicator for the Aintree betting, and Go Ballistic headed the reformed market at 7/1.

The most striking horse in the field was the athletic Suny Bay, a big grey that had won the Greenhalls Grand National Trial at Haydock Park. Trained by Charlie Brooks, Suny Bay was at his best on softer ground, and with the ground drying out considerably, the quick surface was deemed unlikely to produce a win for this horse. Even so, the talented chaser started second best in the betting at 8/1. Nathen Lad and Smith's Band were a strongly fancied duo from the Jenny Pitman yard. Nathen Lad had beaten the recent Gold Cup winner Mr Mulligan in the previous season's Royal & Sun Alliance Chase at the Cheltenham Festival and was a popular each-way selection, while the promising nine-year-old Smith's Band was the choice of jockey Richard Dunwoody, seeking his third Grand National win.

The Irish challenge was headed by Wylde Hide and Feathered Gale. Owned by J.P. McManus, Wylde Hide had been in contention when losing his rider at the second Canal Turn in the previous National and, after winning his latest race, found himself third in the betting at 11/1. Feathered Gale was a horse that was expected to relish the quicker going at Aintree. The horse was a former winner of the Irish Grand National and had finished a creditable sixth in the season's Hennessy Gold Cup.

Among the other interesting contenders for the 1997 race were Master Oats, General Wolfe, Avro Anson and Lord Gyllene. Apart from finishing third in the previous season's King George VI Chase, top-weight Master Oats had failed to recapture the scintillating form of his 1995 Gold Cup win and had been pulled up on his only start of the season in the Ericsson Chase in Ireland, while Lorcan Wyer's mount General Wolfe, a former runner-up in the Scottish Grand National, was attempting to give Captain Tim Forster his fourth National success as a trainer. Avro Anson had run in only six previous chases but, trained by Maurice Camacho, he was expected to love the going and had run well in the Peter Marsh Chase at Haydock Park earlier in the season; another who seemed destined to thrive on such conditions was the New Zealand-bred Lord Gyllene, three times a winner during the season and runner-up on his latest start to the progressive Seven Towers in the Midlands Grand National at Uttoxeter.

Lord Gyllene leads the way as the race finally gets underway on Monday afternoon.

As the runners were called into line for what was, in its own resounding way, a monumental occasion, the legendary commentator, Peter O'Sullevan, prepared to call his fiftieth and final Grand National. As the field set off, Lord Gyllene quickly swept into prominence down the inside, and he shaded the lead over the first fence from Suny Bay and Smith's Band. The only faller at the opening obstacle was Full Of Oats, and as they streamed over the next line of fences, outsider Northern Hide joined the three leaders as they squared up to Becher's Brook. With Lord Gyllene setting the standard, every horse flew majestically over the famous fence, and it was not until the Foinavon fence that the next casualties occurred, with Back Bar falling and Glemot unseating Simon McNeill. Lord Gyllene was jumping beautifully out in front and, behind him, there was very little change, with only Nathen Lad and Dextra Dove moving forward on the inside and outside respectively, although Nuaffe crashed out at the eleventh when beginning to enter the equation.

As they came back onto the racecourse, dramatic incidents began to occur. First of all, the fancied Wylde Hide made a terrible mistake when he all but fell at the thirteenth. A fence later, Straight Talk, partnered by young amateur Joe Tizzard, tragically suffered a fatal, leg-breaking fall. Then, as he began to creep into contention, Celtic Abbey unseated his rider after a horrendous blunder at the Chair, and the string of dramas were rounded off a fence later when a loose horse almost wiped out Lord Gyllene's hopes at the Water. Having received his share of luck by narrowly avoiding disaster moments earlier, Lord Gyllene set about dominating on the second circuit. With Smith's Band, Suny Bay and the improving Master Oats his most serious challengers, he led the field on to Becher's again. The dark side of the National was sadly highlighted once more at the twentieth fence as, after jumping heroically for over a circuit, Smith's Band plunged to the ground and broke his neck in a shuddering fatal fall when still disputing the lead.

Lord Gyllene was growing in confidence with every jump, and as Suny Bay and Master Oats broke clear of the chasing pack – including the faltering favourite Go Ballistic – the three horses had the race to themselves as they crossed the Melling Road for the final time.

As Tony Dobbin drove the strapping New Zealand-bred horse strongly round the home turn, it became clear that only a fall would cost Lord Gyllene victory. Jumping the last two fences in great style, the horse powered on past the elbow and crossed the finishing line an emphatic winner by a full twenty-five lengths. Suny Bay had run a brave race on unfavourable ground, but could not live with the winner and finished a distant second, with outsiders Camelot Knight and Buckboard Bounce coming through to take the minor places. Master Oats, with far more weight to carry than any other horse, had run a race of courage and class, eventually finishing a gallant fifth.

Lord Gyllene's success came for his owner Mr Stan Clark, the chairman of both Uttoxeter and Newcastle racecourses, who had proven his ability for spotting a good horse after purchasing Lord Gyllene on the evidence of videotape from his form in New Zealand. Winning trainer Steve Brookshaw came from a family with National pedigree. Steve's uncle, Tim, had finished second on Wyndburgh in the 1959 race, and now that rider's nephew had gone one better with a horse ridden by the excellent Tony Dobbin. With the 1997 Grand National finally in the record books, everyone associated with the race could feel proud with what had been achieved. Under the most extreme circumstances, the spirit of Aintree had come shining through to further enhance the National's legendary status.

HORSE/FATE	AGE/WEIGHT	JOCKEY	ODDS
1st **LORD GYLLENE**	9.10-0	**A. DOBBIN**	**14/1**
2nd **SUNY BAY**	8.10-3	**J. OSBORNE**	**8/1**
3rd **CAMELOT KNIGHT**	11.10-0	**C. LLEWELLYN**	**100/1**
4th **BUCKBOARD BOUNCE**	11.10-1	**P. CARBERRY**	**40/1**
5th Master Oats	11.11-10	N. Williamson	25/1
6th Avro Anson	9.10-3	P. Niven	12/1
7th Killeshin	11.10-0	S. Curran	33/1
8th Dakyns Boy	12.10-0	T.J. Murphy	100/1
9th Nathen Lad	8.10-9	J.F. Titley	14/1
10th Valiant Warrior	9.10-3	R. Garritty	50/1
11th Antonin	9.10-0	C. O'Dwyer	14/1
12th Northern Hide	11.10-1	P. Holley	66/1
13th Turning Trix	10.10-0	J.R. Kavanagh	25/1
14th Pink Gin	10.10-0	Mr C. Bonner	100/1
15th New Co	9.10-0	D.J. Casey	40/1
16th General Wolfe	8.10-0	L. Wyer	16/1
17th Evangelica	7.10-0	R. Supple	33/1
Lo Stregone - *Pulled Up*	11.10-4	G. Bradley	14/1
Feathered Gale - *Pulled Up*	10.10-3	F. Woods	16/1
Bishops Hall - *Pulled Up*	11.10-1	M. Richards	50/1
Wylde Hide - *Unseated Rider*	10.10-0	C. Swan	11/1
Dextra Dove - *Pulled Up*	10.10-0	C. Maude	33/1
Smith's Band - *Fell*	9.10-2	R. Dunwoody	12/1
Go Ballistic - *Pulled Up*	8.10-3	M.A. Fitzgerald	7/1*
Glemot - *Unseated Rider*	9.10-0	S. McNeill	50/1
Straight Talk - *Fell*	10.10-0	Mr J. Tizzard	50/1
Nuaffe - *Fell*	12.10-0	T. Mitchell	100/1
River Mandate - *Pulled Up*	10.10-1	A. Thornton	50/1
Grange Brake - *Refused*	11.10-4	D. Walsh	100/1
Back Bar - *Fell*	9.10-0	T.P .Treacy	100/1
Scribbler - *Pulled Up*	11.10-2	D. Fortt	100/1
Celtic Abbey - *Unseated Rider*	9.10-0	R. Johnson	66/1
Full Of Oats - *Fell*	11.10-0	J. Culloty	33/1
Mugoni Beach - *Pulled Up*	12.10-0	G. Tormey	100/1
Don't Light Up - *Fell*	11.10-0	Mr R. Thornton	100/1
Spuffington - *Unseated Rider*	9.10-2	P. Hide	100/1

1998
EARTH SUMMIT

After what had happened at Aintree in 1997, the security surrounding the course was extremely tight for the 1998 Grand National meeting, with no cars allowed on the premises. With the heavens opening on the track itself, this National promised to be a supreme test of stamina and courage.

One horse especially appreciative of Aintree's spring weather was the tough ten-year-old Earth Summit. Owned by a syndicate of six, named The Summit Partnership, it could be argued that the horse was enjoying a reincarnation of a once very promising career. Having won the Scottish Grand National as a six-year-old, Earth Summit had looked every inch a future Grand National winner until injury severely disrupted the next few years of his career; at one point, it looked unlikely that he would ever race again. But under the guidance of trainer Nigel Twiston-Davies, the horse had rocketed back to life with a battling win in the Welsh Grand National at Chepstow earlier in the season, and with conditions equally, if not more heavy, at Aintree, Earth Summit was made a late favourite for the race at 7/1. To encourage his backers further, the horse had on board the winning jockey from 1992, Carl Llewellyn, and just as on that occasion, he replaced an injured colleague, this time Tom Jenks.

The horse Earth Summit replaced at the head of the betting was the 1996 winner, Rough Quest, who was back after missing Lord Gyllene's race through injury. Terry Casey's horse had kept top-class company in his recent chases, and on his latest start in the Cheltenham Gold Cup, he had been travelling strongly until suffering a rare fall behind surprise winner Cool Dawn. However, not lost on the public was his thoroughly convincing win in the 1996 National, and although the heavy ground had somewhat subdued his chances, Mick Fitzgerald's mount still started 11/1 in the betting.

On the same mark was the twelve-stone carrying top weight, Suny Bay. The big grey horse had enjoyed a most impressive season, the highlight being a total destruction of a high quality field in the valuable Hennessy Gold Cup at Newbury. Ridden this time by Graham Bradley, Suny Bay was facing a battle against the history books, as no horse had won the National under a twelve-stone burden since the one and only Red Rum in 1974.

Of the newcomers to the race, one that had risen to prominence in the preceding months was the sometimes lazy, but sound-jumping stayer Him Of Praise. Oliver Sherwood's contender had registered his National credentials with a quartet of chase wins earlier in the season and had run consistently, if temperamentally, since. Despite his trainer's fear that, at the age of eight, the horse may be too young for the supreme test, Him Of Praise appealed to many as he was very lightly weighted and suited to the arduous challenge that lay ahead in the testing conditions. Like Earth Summit, he came in for a lot of late support to start at 8/1.

Among the thirty-seven runners, Samlee, Challenger Du Luc, Dun Belle and Ciel De Brion stood out as most interesting of the remaining competitors. Samlee had a fine record in long distance chases, having been placed in both Scottish and Welsh Grand

Nationals, and had performed admirably over the big fences to win the Becher Chase earlier in the season, while Challenger Du Luc was the real wild card of the race, being an undeniably strong competitor but also, on occasions, reluctant – as he showed when throwing away a certain victory in the King George VI Chase earlier in the season through an apparent unwillingness to battle. The mare Dun Belle was the most fancied of a relatively weak Irish challenge and had finished an excellent second to the fine chaser Doran's Pride in the Irish Hennessy Gold Cup on her penultimate race before Aintree, while French raider Ciel De Brion was trained by the highly respected François Doumen and ridden by his son, Thierry.

Despite the heavy conditions, the sun shone brightly as the runners were called into line. Without any hesitation from the starter, they were sent on their way and, making a surprisingly brisk charge on the boggy surface, the field came towards the first fence.

The fancied Him Of Praise was among the first to rise in the centre of the track, together with the Irish mare Dun Belle, while Scotton Banks stuck to the inside rail. The first shock arrived swiftly as Martin Pipe's Challenger Du Luc crashed awkwardly on the landing side, while Pashto, Diwali Dancer, What A Hand and Banjo all came to grief at the opening obstacle.

More spills followed soon after as the slow-starting Fabricator came down at the big third fence and then Do Rightly crashed to the floor, having clipped the fourth hard. With Griffins Bar another casualty at the fifth flight, the field was already greatly reduced by the time Becher's Brook came into sight.

With Him Of Praise, Greenhill Tare Away, Decyborg, Dun Belle and Ciel De Brion leading into the mighty fence, the early exodus from the race continued as Court Melody and Choisty both fell on the inside, leaving their respective jockeys, Timmy Murphy and Richard McGrath, lying splattered in the muddy turf.

At Valentine's Brook, Dun Belle, in contention on the outside, made a bad blunder and unseated her rider, while up front two of the outsiders, Greenhill Tare Away and Decyborg, had pulled clear of the chasing pack and, as they started to slow the pace down somewhat, they bounded across the Melling Road and back onto the racecourse.

With the runners in clear view of the packed grandstand, a loose horse very nearly brought havoc to the race when it darted across the path of the leaders approaching the fourteenth fence. Fortunately, the rider-less animal had a sudden change of mind and proceeded to jump the obstacle, allowing the French raider Ciel De Brion to assume command over the Chair and Water.

The field was beginning to become ruthlessly strung-out, as the heavy ground wore down a whole host of stragglers. As the second circuit began, many tired runners cried enough and pulled up. For those left standing, it was going to be an enormous test of stamina to last home. Still at the head of affairs, Greenhill Tare Away and Ciel De Brion were showing no signs of letting up, while the fancied trio of Earth Summit, Suny Bay and Rough Quest were slowly but surely creeping into the action.

At the big ditch, Ciel De Brion made a bad mistake, but with his young jockey Thierry Doumen enjoying a fabulous first ride in the National, they survived to reclaim a

The heavy conditions suited the robust Earth Summit in 1998.

prominent position at the second Becher's, with Greenhill Tare Away running the race of his life in the middle, Earth Summit on the wide outside and Rough Quest and Suny Bay poised behind.

One by one, the challengers were dropping away. At the Canal Turn, the lightly weighted Brave Highlander, running in the famous white and blue Aldaniti colours, unshipped his rider after improving his position, and soon after, Rough Quest, who was not enjoying the gruelling conditions, began to tire. Then, five fences from home, Ciel De Brion paid the price for a slow jump and Greenhill Tare Away's brave effort came to a halt a fence later when he unseated Simon McNeill. With Him Of Praise refusing further back, process of elimination meant that Earth Summit and Suny Bay had the race to themselves; crossing the Melling Road for a final time, they pulled well clear of the few remaining participants.

Matching strides as they approached the second last, it was obvious that the big weight difference was going to play a major role in the outcome and, separated by 23lb, the less-burdened Earth Summit gradually began to edge ahead.

After jumping the last, the race seemed to continue in super-slow motion as the blinkered Earth Summit dug as deep as he could into his reserves of stamina. Suny Bay, who had been as white as the beard of Father Christmas before the race, was now chocolate coloured, and as bravely as he tried, he simply could not force his way past Earth Summit, and the favourite went on to give Carl Llewellyn his second National victory in the most exhausting of performances.

Suny Bay was as gallant a runner-up as the race had ever witnessed, and it was an illustration of just how well the first two had performed in the treacherous conditions when the next finishers, Samlee and St Mellion Fairway, came home an age later. Only Gimme Five and the remounted Killeshin also completed the course in a race considered even more gruelling than when Miinnehoma won in 1994. Sadly, three horses had been killed in the very early stages, although the heavy ground was not blamed for the tragic losses of Pashto, Do Rightly and Griffins Bar.

Earth Summit triumphed in courageous style and once more proved his incredible liking for a thorough test of stamina. The victory captured a fantastic hat-trick for the winner, with the Grand National now added to his triumphs in the Scottish and Welsh equivalents.

Watching as an analyst live on national television was Peter Scudamore, the former champion jump jockey who was now assistant trainer to Nigel Twiston Davies. Scudamore had never managed to win the great race as a jockey, but the emotion he showed in front of millions proved what it meant to be part of a winning team in the famous spectacle.

Also captured on camera during wild, post-race celebrations were members of The Summit Partnership, including Aintree press officer Nigel Payne and former footballer Ricky George. The syndicate members had always dreamed of Grand National victory for their beloved Earth Summit, despite all his injury problems. Now that dream had come true in glorious fashion.

HORSE/FATE	AGE/WEIGHT	JOCKEY	ODDS
1st **EARTH SUMMIT**	10.10-5	**C. LLEWELLYN**	**7/1***
2nd **SUNY BAY**	9.12-0	**G. BRADLEY**	**11/1**
3rd **SAMLEE**	9.10-1	**R. DUNWOODY**	**8/1**
4th **ST MELLION FAIRWAY**	9.10-1	**A. THORNTON**	**20/1**
5th Gimme Five	11.10-0	K. Whelan	25/1
6th Killeshin	12.10-0	S. Curran - *Remount*	25/1
Rough Quest - *Pulled Up*	12.11-4	M.A. Fitzgerald	11/1
Challenger Du Luc - *Fell*	8.11-3	A.P. McCoy	12/1
Scotton Banks -*Unseated Rider*	9.10-7	L. Wyer	33/1
Banjo - *Fell*	8.10-7	R. Johnson	14/1
Nathen Lad - *Fell*	9.10-3	R. Farrant	13/1
Dun Belle - *Unseated Rider*	9.10-0	T.P. Treacy	18/1
General Crack - *Pulled Up*	9.10-1	Mr J. Tizzard	40/1
Go Universal - *Pulled Up*	10.10-0	Mr S. Durack	66/1
Ciel De Brion - *Fell*	8.10-0	T. Doumen	16/1
Court Melody - *Fell*	10.10-0	T.J. Murphy	25/1
Celtic Abbey - *Fell*	10.10-0	N. Williamson	33/1
Him Of Praise - *Refused*	8.10-0	C. Swan	8/1
Into The Red - *Pulled Up*	14.10-0	D. Gallagher	50/1
What A Hand - *Fell*	10.10-0	C. Maude	66/1
Greenhill Tare Away - *Unseated Rider*	10.10-0	S. McNeill	100/1
Yeoman Warrior - *Pulled Up*	11.10-1	Richard Guest	100/1
Pond House - *Pulled Up*	9.10-0	T. Dascombe	66/1
Brave Highlander - *Unseated Rider*	10.10-0	P. Hide	25/1
Hillwalk - *Pulled Up*	12.10-0	Mr R.Wakley	150/1
Joe White - *Pulled Up*	12.10-0	Mr T. McCarthy	150/1
Diwali Dancer - *Fell*	8.10-0	R. Thornton	100/1
Do Rightly - *Fell*	9.10-0	P. Holley	100/1
Fabricator - *Fell*	12.10-0	J. Supple	150/1
Pashto - *Fell*	11.10-0	J.R. Kavanagh	100/1
Radical Choice - *Pulled Up*	9.10-0	B. Storey	66/1
Damas - *Refused*	7.10-0	Jamie Evans	200/1
Choisty - *Fell*	8.10-0	R. McGrath	40/1
Griffins Bar - *Fell*	10.10-0	G. Tormey	200/1
Winter Belle - *Pulled Up*	10.10-0	Mr C. Bonner	100/1
Maple Dancer - *Pulled Up*	12.10-0	G. Shenkin	200/1
Decyborg - *Pulled Up*	7.10-0	P. Carberry	200/1

1999
BOBBYJO

Although the field for the 1999 Grand National again fell well short of the maximum number of runners, with only thirty-two lining up for battle, there was a highly competitive feel to the event as, unusually, a high percentage of the horses stood a realistic chance of winning or being at least being placed.

Ever since the publication of the National weights, one horse in particular had stood out from the rest. Owned by Mr Reg Wilkins, who had held a strong fancy in 1994 with Double Silk, the horse was the emerging nine-year-old Double Thriller. With 10st 8lb to carry, Double Thriller had the appearance of a handicap snip, for the former hunter-chaser had gone from strength to strength during the season. Having joined the powerful Paul Nicholls stable at the beginning of his campaign, the horse had won his opening pair of races to confirm his status as a horse with limitless potential, before being thrown in with the big guns in the Cheltenham Gold Cup. Letting nobody down, Double Thriller led for a long way until finally finishing fourth to stablemate See More Business, but he had marked himself down as a major contender for Aintree, where he would be ridden by teenager Joe Tizzard. On the day, it looked as though Double Thriller would start as one of the shortest priced favourites ever, as many punters had him doubled with the recent Lincoln Handicap winner Right Wing. As the race drew closer, he eventually eased from a ridiculously short 9/2 to a starting price of 7/1.

Amazingly, after weeks of hype, Double Thriller did not go off favourite, and the Grand National market leader on this occasion was, most unusually, a mare, the tough and consistent Fiddling The Facts. One of the reasons for her popularity stemmed from her supercharged stable, where trainer Nicky Henderson was enjoying a marvellous season and jockey Mick Fitzgerald was fresh from the winning ride in the Gold Cup. Never out of the first three in her fours runs during the season, Fiddling The Facts had proved her stamina when finishing strongly to take second in the Welsh Grand National at Chepstow. With a flood of race-day support, the mare proudly started as the 6/1 favourite. Having won a Whitbread Gold Cup the previous season, Call It A Day possessed a touch of class, and the reliable jumper and stayer had long been considered an ideal candidate for the Grand National. The horse – more fancied than trainer David Nicholson's second runner, the Scottish Grand National winner Baronet – had Richard Dunwoody in the saddle, who had already won two Nationals and been placed in five others. With the good ground in Call It A Day's favour, the horse, also third in an Irish Grand National, started a very popular 7/1.

After slugging out the finish to one of the most punishing Nationals in recent years the season before, Earth Summit and Suny Bay were back to renew their rivalry in far less testing conditions. Earth Summit was the only former Grand National winner running on this occasion, as the impressive 1997 victor Lord Gyllene was again ruled out through injury. Earth Summit had once more proved his affection for the big Aintree fences, easily winning the Becher Chase earlier in the season, but after a number of disappointing runs since, and with 11st to carry, the 1998 hero took a cluster of lingering doubts into battle with him.

Similarly, Suny Bay had struggled in his recent races after an encouraging start to his campaign, and had recently thrown in a poor effort in the Gold Cup. Even so, now trained by Simon Sherwood, Suny Bay had earned an army of supporters following his brave effort in the 1998 National, and once again he was very popular in the betting, starting at 12/1.

Eudipe, Nathen Lad and Bobbyjo were fascinating contenders in a wide-open Grand National. Eudipe was considered to be star jockey Tony McCoy's best chance so far of winning the race, and the game seven-year-old had run competitively in a host of top staying chases, including the Scottish Grand National and Hennessy Gold Cup. There would have been no more popular winner than Nathen Lad, who was the last ever National representative for the first lady of Aintree, Jenny Pitman, while Bobbyjo, a former winner of the Irish Grand National, was looking to end Ireland's frustrating twenty-four year wait for a National success and was the subject of a monstrous late plunge of money – starting at 10/1, having been available at twice those odds in the morning.

With clear blue sky welcoming the start of another great spectacle, the eager field was dispatched by starter Simon Morant, and they thundered away towards the first of thirty, spruce-covered obstacles.

With the yellow-blinkered Cyborgo, one of four hopefuls for Martin Pipe, narrowly leading in the middle from Blue Charm, General Wolfe and Nathen Lad, the runners met the first fence. With a collection of outstanding jumps from the leading group, it appeared

Blue Charm (21) led for a long way in 1999.

at first as though the opening flight would, unlike the previous year, escape drama-free. However, to the shock of everyone, the highly touted Double Thriller, having over-jumped badly, crashed to the turf and provided a major anti-climax to his pre-National hype.

The dark grey, Baronet, was being held up towards the rear by Richard Johnson and had been jumping quite well, but the fourth fence was his downfall as he cascaded to the ground in an ugly spill. The remaining thirty stayed upright as they continued down to Becher's Brook, with the Scottish-based Blue Charm leading along with General Wolfe.

As they sailed over the Brook, Nathen Lad nearly brought a premature end to Jenny Pitman's interest as he skidded dangerously on the landing side before recovering, but for Tamarindo and the disinterested veteran Mudahim, the famous fence proved their undoing.

Blue Charm, running from well out of the handicap, was beginning to settle into a comfortable rhythm up front, and together with General Wolfe, he dictated proceedings over Valentine's Brook and the fences out in the country. Outsider Feels Like Gold was also enjoying his first experience of the unique fences and, with Nathen Lad still close enough to tantalise those hoping for a fairytale result, they came back onto the racecourse with plenty still in the race.

Taking the Chair, Blue Charm was cruising and giving Lorcan Wyer a dream ride – which he had only picked up as a replacement for the injured amateur Mark Bradburne. Meanwhile, former Aintree Foxhunter's winner Cavalero had made a blunder at the four-

Paul Carberry unleashed Bobbyjo break Ireland's twenty-four year National hoodoo.

teenth which caused jockey Sean Curran's saddle to slip to such an extent that the outsider was forced out of the contest before the Chair.

With a tremendously competitive contest warming up, the runners embarked on their second circuit with Blue Charm and his long-time companions General Wolfe, Feels Like Gold and Nathen Lad still very much in contention; behind them, Brave Highlander, Samlee and the fancied pair of Fiddling The Facts and Eudipe were all mounting serious challenges.

As with so many previous Grand Nationals, the second Becher's Brook was to have a resounding impact on the destiny of the race. Moving ominously on the tails of the leaders, the favourite, Fiddling The Facts, hit the deck and the improving Frazer Island also crashed down. Worse was to come as the gutsy Eudipe suffered a tragic, back-breaking fall when right in contention, and with Camelot Knight and Choisty also eliminated from the race, Becher's had again risen to its still fearsome reputation. Lorcan Wyer was still going extremely well on 25/1 shot Blue Charm, and with the previous year's principals Earth Summit and Suny Bay both struggling to keep up with the pace, he led a band of eight challengers, who made a break for glory crossing the Melling Road for a final time. As well as the leader, closely grouped now were Brave Highlander, Bobbyjo, Call It A Day, Feels Like Gold, Merry People, Nathen Lad and Addington Boy.

Rounding the turn for home, Philip Hide pushed Brave Highlander onto the shoulders of the long-time leader, and as he did so, Richard Dunwoody rushed Call It A Day through to challenge, sparking roars of encouragement from the crowd. At the second last, Jenny Pitman's dream exit was extinguished as Nathen Lad, together with Feels Like Gold, saw their challenges evaporate, but conversely, Irish eyes were widening coming to the fence, as both Bobbyjo and Merry People were moving strongly on the outside. Then, suddenly, Merry People was on the floor and he almost took his fellow Irish raider with him, such was the closeness of the two horses. Receiving a big slice of luck, Bobbyjo loomed dangerously behind the leaders at the final fence, where Call It A Day and Blue Charm were hanging on grimly in dispute of first place, while Brave Highlander's bid was rapidly fading. Encouraged by rapturous Irish voices, and those that had helped to spark the late gamble on the horse, Paul Carberry quickly accelerated Bobbyjo into a lead approaching the elbow. Try as he might and fighting back with all his heart, Blue Charm could not regain his initiative and Call It A Day likewise failed to match the blistering late surge of the Irish horse.

Emphatically ending Ireland's twenty-four year wait for a Grand National winner, Bobbyjo sprinted over the line to give Paul Carberry the biggest win of his life. The game Blue Charm, considered a doubtful stayer before the race, defiantly held onto second place with Call It A Day giving Dunwoody another memorable Aintree ride in third. Addington Boy stayed on for fourth with Nathen Lad finishing the final Jenny Pitman chapter pleasingly, coming home safely in eleventh. Bobbyjo had succeeded where many others had tried and failed. He had given the Irish a long overdue victory with a perfectly timed run under a highly talented young rider in Paul Carberry. What made the victory even sweeter was that the horse, owned by Mr Robert Burke, was trained by Paul's father, Tommy – himself a winning rider on the last Irish victor, L'Escargot, in 1975. They became the first father and son to triumph since Reg and Bruce Hobbs won with Battleship in 1938, and only the sixth successful duo ever. With Irish eyes smiling all over Aintree, the one question that remained unanswered was; how long would it be until the next victory for the Emerald Isle?

HORSE/FATE	AGE/WEIGHT	JOCKEY	ODDS
1st **BOBBYJO**	9.10-0	P. CARBERRY	10/1
2nd **BLUE CHARM**	9.10-0	L. WYER	25/1
3rd **CALL IT A DAY**	9.10-2	R. DUNWOODY	7/1
4th **ADDINGTON BOY**	11.10-7	A. MAGUIRE	10/1
5th Feels Like Gold	11.10-0	B. Harding	50/1
6th Brave Highlander	11.10-1	P. Hide	50/1
7th Kendal Cavalier	9.10-0	B. Fenton	28/1
8th Earth Summit	11.11-0	C. Llewellyn	16/1
9th St Mellion Fairway	10.10-2	J. Frost	200/1
10th Samlee	10.10-0	R. Farrant	50/1
11th Nathen Lad	10.10-2	A. Thornton	14/1
12th General Wolfe	10.11-1	N. Williamson	18/1
13th Suny Bay	10.11-13	G. Bradley	12/1
14th Back Bar	11.10-0	D. Gallagher	200/1
15th Strong Chairman	8.10-0	R. Thornton	50/1
16th Merry People	11.10-0	G. Cotter - *Remount*	200/1
17th Avro Anson	11.10-0	A. Dobbin	40/1
18th Coome Hill	10.10-11	S. Wynne	25/1
Cyborgo - *Pulled Up*	9.10-11	C. O'Dwyer	50/1
Eudipe - *Fell*	7.10-10	A.P. McCoy	10/1
Double Thriller - *Fell*	9.10-8	J. Tizzard	7/1
Tamarindo - *Fell*	6.10-4	T.J. Murphy	66/1
Fiddling The Facts - *Fell*	8.10-3	M.A. Fitzgerald	6/1*
Baronet - *Fell*	9.10-2	R. Johnson	12/1
Bells Life - *Pulled Up*	10.10-0	G. Tormey	66/1
Mudahim - *Unseated Rider*	13.10-0	B. Powell	100/1
Commercial Artist - *Pulled Up*	13.10-2	T. Jenks	200/1
Frazer Island - *Fell*	10.10-2	Richard Guest	200/1
Camelot Knight - *Brought Down*	13.10-0	C. Maude	200/1
Cavalero - *Pulled Up*	10.10-0	S. Curran	50/1
Castle Coin - *Unseated Rider*	7.10-0	A.S. Smith	200/1
Choisty - *Unseated Rider*	9.10-0	R. Widger	200/1

2000
PAPILLON

Even more so than the highly competitive race of a year before, the first Grand National of the new millennium attracted a plethora of highly capable runners, resulting in one of the most open contests of all time. With the well structured assessment of race handicapper Phil Smith, an incredible thirty-three of the forty horses in the field ran from inside the handicap, presenting the National with its first maximum turnout since 1992.

As punters around the country found themselves with an endless array of enticing candidates to place their money on, it was one of thirty newcomers to the race that eventually started favourite after a feverish betting contest. The participant in question was the Martin Pipe-trained nine-year-old Dark Stranger, the mount of champion jockey Tony McCoy. The horse was, in some respects, a surprise market leader as he had never won beyond three miles, but he had been most impressive when capturing the Mildmay of Flete Chase at the recent Cheltenham Festival. Having responded notably to the fitting of blinkers on that occasion, Dark Stranger again carried the headgear for his assault on Aintree and with his ever-popular team guiding him, the horse was to start at 9/1.

Several other horses had flirted with favouritism for the 2000 Grand National at one time or another. One of those was the exuberant Henry Daly-trained Star Traveller. Consistency was the little horse's forte, and already with a pair of wins earlier in the season, arguably his best performance had come on his latest start, when he had run extremely well behind one of the most improved and talented horses in the country, Marlborough, at the Cheltenham Festival. So far, in a rising career, the Grand National had not been too kind on Richard Johnson, but Star Traveller was deemed his best ride in the race to date. Despite the fears that the horse would be too small to combat Aintree's huge fences, Star Traveller began the race as a well-supported 10/1 chance.

After finally ending Ireland's drought in the previous year's National, Bobbyjo returned to Aintree with another milestone in his sights. Not since Red Rum in 1974 had a Grand National winner recorded a second consecutive victory in the race, but Bobbyjo was strongly fancied to break the trend. Having run well over hurdles on his most recent outing, the horse again found his favoured good ground waiting for him at Aintree, while Paul Carberry had sufficiently recovered from an injury to take his place on board the 12/1 shot. If there was a doubt concerning Bobbyjo on this occasion, it was the fact that he had risen substantially in the weights and now had to shoulder a hefty 11st 6lb.

In one of the biggest late gambles in the entire history of the Grand National, another Irish contender, Papillon, became the hottest property on the day of the race, cutting through the betting market like a shark through water. After being heavily tipped on an eve-of-race television programme by a number of racing journalists and again on the morning of the race in national newspapers, Papillon's odds simply kept on shrinking. Despite being a former runner-up to Bobbyjo in an Irish Grand National, his recent form in Ireland had been poor, but that was put down to the fact he was carrying impossible weights on unfavourable soft ground. But after a pleasing third in a hurdles race on good ground, Ted

Walsh's horse found himself with both suitable going and a lighter weight at Aintree, and having been generally available at 33/1 on the morning of the race, Papillon incredibly went off at 10/1.

In an intensely competitive field, some of the eye-catching runners included Micko's Dream, Earthmover, Young Kenny and Mely Moss. Eight-year-old Micko's Dream was owned by twenty-four Irish prison officers and had stamped his Grand National intentions down when impressively winning the Thyestes Chase in Ireland earlier in the season and was a fast-improving horse, while Earthmover headed a team of four for Paul Nicholls. The former Cheltenham Foxhunter's winner was another that came in for late support, eventually starting at 14/1. Young Kenny had been the most improved chaser in training the previous season, racking up a string of top quality staying events, including the Scottish Grand National. The big, athletic horse had long been considered an ideal type for Aintree, while Mely Moss, who had not been raced all season, had been second in the previous year's Aintree Foxhunter's and been trained by Charlie Egerton with the Grand National meeting in mind.

An overcast afternoon created a dull backdrop to the big race, but as the forty runners prepared for the start, the colourful mixture of bright jockey's silks and supremely fit horses was enough to bring the whole of Aintree to life, as the bubbly crowd waited with excitement for the race to unfold.

They did not have long to wait as the field literally thundered towards the first fence on the lush green turf. The Norwegian Grand National winner and complete outsider, Trinitro, was charging furiously at the obstacle, with jockey Robert Bellamy fighting to keep the

Locked together at the last – Papillon (right) and Mely Moss.

horse at a sensible pace, and they just led in the middle of the track, with Torduff Express, Esprit De Cotte and Bobbyjo right up there as they confronted their first challenge.

Rising like a salmon, the Norwegian challenger paid for his exuberance by crashing dramatically to the floor, while on the inside rail, the fancied Micko's Dream similarly over-jumped and bit the dust. The frantic dash to the first had wiped out an eighth of the field, with two of the Martin Pipe runners, Art Prince and Royal Predica, together with the popular grey Senor El Betrutti, also coming to grief.

There was to be no let-up in the blistering pace or the flamboyant exits. At the second, Sparky Gayle, a one-time Cheltenham Gold Cup hope, departed the race, and the usual groans from the crowd were evident as the favourite Dark Stranger left his back legs in the third, unseating Tony McCoy and ending Martin Pipe's hopes of adding to Miinnehoma's nail-biting win in 1994.

By the time they faced up to Becher's Brook, both Earthmover and, for the third time in the Grand National, Choisty, had come down, and it was the front-running Star Traveller who had taken up the lead, together with Bobbyjo, Esprit De Cotte and Torduff Express.

With most of the field clearing Becher's with scintillating leaps, only Red Marauder, a horse whom his jockey Richard Guest had been particularly confident in, was a casualty as he skidded to the ground at the back of the field after a number of sketchy jumps at the previous fences.

After Bobbyjo survived a horrendous mistake at the Foinavon fence, Star Traveller assumed command and, jumping boldly, he headed Esprit De Cotte as the field streamed over the Canal Turn and Valentine's Brook. However, back in the field on the wide outside, Young Kenny's Grand National dreams were wrecked at the tenth fence, as the strapping chaser somersaulted out of the action.

Coming back onto the racecourse, Paul Nicholls' runner Torduff Express, wearing a sheepskin noseband, had moved strongly into a leading position, but miscalculating the thirteenth, the 50/1 shot crumbled to the floor, while a fence later, little Star Traveller gave his followers a worrying moment when making a hash of the obstacle.

Surviving his blunder, Star Traveller held his position over the Chair and Water, and gamely led out for the second circuit, closely attended by Esprit De Cotte, The Last Fling, Papillon, Lucky Town, Brave Highlander and Addington Boy.

With Village King the only close-up challenger to come down on the run to Becher's for a second time, the leaders were still tantalisingly well grouped approaching this critical stage of the race, with another Irish raider in Hollybank Buck – a former Eider Chase winner – moving strongly into contention.

Esprit De Cotte, having been up with the pace the whole time, misjudged the deceiving drop and fell, together with Stormy Passage (who carried the famous blue and black colours associated with Aintree legend West Tip) and the duo's falls proceeded to interfere with the progress of Bobbyjo, virtually vanquishing the 1999 winner's hopes of a repeat win.

Papillon, the huge last-minute gamble, struck the front at the Canal Turn as, for the first time, the plucky Star Traveller came under pressure, while further back but improving, Buck Rogers hurtled to the turf and gave his jockey Ken Whelan a bumpy exit. After Star Traveller hit Valentine's hard, resulting in him being pulled up two fences later, Papillon began to impose his physical strength on the race and, jumping brilliantly, he led a large number of horses down the back and across the Melling Road for a final time.

The challengers were circling like vultures around Papillon, with Brave Highlander, Lucky Town, Niki Dee, Addington Boy and Mely Moss all close enough to strike a deadly blow to the Irish leader. But as Lucky Town faded and Brave Highlander made a mistake at the second last, Papillon suddenly had just one rival to shake off approaching the final flight.

Moving imperiously well on his inside, Norman Williamson had ghosted Mely Moss through to severely threaten the leader, but with extreme strength, Papillon flew clear after jumping the fence and bounded on towards the elbow.

With thrilling determination, Mely Moss responded with a surge that seemed certain to produce victory as the two entered the closing stages, but such was the desire and whole-hearted grit of Papillon that the Irish horse prevailed in an electric finale and sent jockey Ruby Walsh in to a burst of delight as they passed the winning post.

It had been a fine achievement by Mely Moss to get so close on his first run of the season and he had been desperately unlucky to come up against an opponent so resolute as Papillon. Niki Dee, stablemate of the fallen Young Kenny, performed admirably to take third in front of Aintree specialist Brave Highlander, deservedly placed after two fine previous efforts in the National.

Not only had the Irish, having waited such a long time for a National winner until 1999's triumph, pulled off the trick again on this occasion, but they had remarkably done it with yet another father and son team, with trainer Ted Walsh and twenty-year-old jockey Ruby Walsh the triumphant pair.

Waiting for them in the winning enclosure was the relieved American owner of Papillon, Mrs Betty Moran. Mrs Moran had harboured serious doubts over the safety of the National fences and had been initially dubious as to whether she should let her horse run in the race. But after a personal inspection, she decided that the course was not as dangerous as it had been illustrated to her. She was rewarded with a superbly brave effort from her equine star, as Papillon landed the mammoth gamble staked on him in the process.

With five horses having been killed on the first two days of the Grand National meeting, it was a fantastic relief for everyone to witness a memorable National with no tragedies and with the Irish achieving another glorious success, Aintree was once more alive with jubilant celebrations, as Papillon was hailed as the first Grand National hero of the millennium.

HORSE/FATE	AGE/WEIGHT	JOCKEY	ODDS
1st **PAPILLON**	**9.10-12**	**R. WALSH**	**10/1**
2nd **MELY MOSS**	**9.10-1**	**N. WILLIAMSON**	**25/1**
3rd **NIKI DEE**	**10.10-13**	**R. SUPPLE**	**25/1**
4th **BRAVE HIGHLANDER**	**12.10-0**	**P. HIDE**	**50/1**
5th Addington Boy	12.11-2	A. Maguire	33/1
6th Call It A Day	10.10-11	B.J. Geraghty	50/1
7th The Last Fling	10.11-5	S. Durack	14/1
8th Lucky Town	9.10-5	D.J. Casey	20/1
9th Djeddah	9.11-8	T. Doumen	16/1
10th Hollybank Buck	10.10-4	P. Niven	33/1
11th Bobbyjo	10.11-6	P. Carberry	12/1
12th Kendal Cavalier	10.10-6	B. Fenton	33/1
13th Suny Bay	11.11-12	C. Maude	66/1
14th Feels Like Gold	12.10-7	B. Harding	28/1
15th Camelot Knight	14.10-0	O. McPhail	150/1
16th Kingdom Of Shades	10.10-4	T. Jenks	50/1
17th Celtic Giant	10.10-0	B. Gibson	100/1
Young Kenny - *Fell*	9.12-0	B. Powell	14/1
Escartefigue - *Unseated Rider*	8.11-9	J.A. McCarthy	50/1
Listen Timmy - *Pulled Up*	11.11-5	A. Dobbin	50/1
Stormy Passage - *Fell*	10.11-3	A. Thornton	50/1
Red Marauder - *Fell*	10.11-2	Richard Guest	18/1
Buck Rogers - *Fell*	11.11-0	K. Whelan	50/1
Senor El Betrutti - *Fell*	11.10-12	C. Llewellyn	100/1
Star Traveller - *Pulled Up*	9.10-11	R. Johnson	10/1
Village King - *Fell*	7.10-11	J. Culloty	50/1
Micko's Dream - *Fell*	8.10-10	J.F. Titley	14/1
Esprit De Cotte - *Fell*	8.10-8	M.A. Fitzgerald	50/1
Sparky Gayle - *Unseated Rider*	10.10-8	B. Storey	33/1
Earthmover - *Fell*	9.10-5	J. Tizzard	14/1
Royal Predica - *Fell*	6.10-4	G. Tormey	50/1
Trinitro - *Fell*	9.10-3	R. Bellamy	100/1
Torduff Express - *Fell*	9.10-3	R. Thornton	50/1
The Gopher - *Fell*	11.10-3	W. Marston	66/1
Dark Stranger - *Unseated Rider*	9.10-1	A.P. McCoy	9/1*
Choisty - *Fell*	10.10-0	R. Widger	50/1
Flaked Oats - *Fell*	11.10-0	T.J. Murphy	50/1
Art Prince - *Fell*	10.10-0	D. Gallagher	100/1
Merry People - *Unseated Rider*	12.10-0	G. Cotter	40/1
Druid's Brook - *Unseated Rider*	11.10-0	R. Wakley	66/1

2001
RED MARAUDER

In recent times, the Grand National had witnessed some extremely testing races on ground that asked the competitors to reach into their furthest reserves of stamina. In particular, Miinnehoma's defiant effort to beat Just So in 1994 and Earth Summit outlasting Suny Bay in the mud in 1998 were races of maximum endurance. But both of those contests paled in comparison to the totally treacherous conditions that greeted the forty hopefuls for the 2001 Grand National. After three days of torrential rain, the stage was set for one of the most extraordinary Nationals ever – one that by its sheer freakish nature will live long in the memory of anyone that saw it.

The disturbing foot-and-mouth crisis that had blitzed the country and reaped havoc on the livelihoods of the nation's farming communities had also greatly disrupted the racing calendar. Only a month previously, the cherished Cheltenham Festival had been lost, and with Irish runners recommended to stay away from Britain, it looked for a long time that the Grand National meeting would lack a key element as well. However, a last minute change of heart saw restrictions lifted and Irish horses allowed to make their journey to Aintree. Although many of their contenders had already withdrawn from the race, the news gave Papillon a chance to bid for a repeat success in the National, with Hollybank Buck and Merry People also venturing over the water, together with a horse recently transferred to England, Inis Cara.

Although the first two in the previous year's race, Papillon and Mely Moss, had dominated the ante-post market for almost twelve months and remained leading contenders, the barrage of rain that had fallen at Aintree prior to the big race had given the betting a complete shake up. Similar to when the ground had turned testing in 1998 and mud-lover Earth Summit rose to become favourite, the betting public searched the field for those that had both buckets of stamina and the ability to handle the going. The result was three co-favourites who all matched the criteria: Edmond, Moral Support and Inis Cara.

Having won the Welsh Grand National two years before, the front-running Edmond, trained by Henry Daly, had proved disappointing since. But now fitted with blinkers, the mud-loving horse could not have had conditions more in his favour and Richard Johnson took his place on the 10/1 shot with renewed confidence. The progressive nine-year-old Moral Support had enjoyed a fine start to his campaign, registering four wins in a row before finishing a brave second in the Welsh Grand National. Trained by Charlie Mann, his chance, like Edmond's, became more enhanced with every drop of rain that fell and Noel Fehily's mount developed into an extremely popular selection on the day. Following a dispute with Irish trainer Michael Hourigan, Inis Cara was sent to the yard of major British trainer Venetia Williams just two days before the race. What the trainer could not of anticipated, however, was that just forty-eight hours later she would be saddling a co-favourite for the Grand National, as Inis Cara went through the same eye-catching nosedive through the odds that Papillon had done the year before. Due to the horse's love for heavy going, Inis Cara, who had been 66/1 earlier in the week, had his price trimmed ferociously to 10/1 as punters latched on to the formula of twelve months before. In truth, Inis Cara had little form in Ireland, with the exception of a third place behind the 2000 Cheltenham Gold Cup winner, Looks Like Trouble, earlier in the season.

Aside from the horses that craved the mud, the horse that captured the most attention was the horse that was undoubtedly the class animal of the race. Beau, an eight-year-old with enormous talent, had posted one of the performances of the previous season with a resounding, all-the-way victory in the Whitbread Gold Cup. Trainer Nigel Twiston-Davies had to vigorously persuade Beau's owner, Mrs Sylvia Tainton, to even run the top weight, but having conceded, Beau was allowed to take his place in the line-up and attempt to give his jockey, Carl Llewellyn, his third win in the race.

Smarty, Blowing Wind and Red Marauder all held sound chances in the war of attrition that awaited them. Smarty, a super jumper and stayer, was the representative of trainer Mark Pitman, who had ridden Garrison Savannah to near victory in 1991, while Blowing Wind was, incredibly, one of a record ten runners for Martin Pipe, and the one selected by his stable jockey, Tony McCoy, for his ability to handle the going. Red Marauder had failed miserably in his first Grand National appearance in 2000, making numerous mistakes before falling at Becher's Brook on the first circuit. He was, however, another horse that appreciated softer ground – which he had not received in the previous year's race – and the contrast in conditions prompted trainer Norman Mason and jockey Richard Guest to have another go on this occasion.

With the rain falling relentlessly as the runners assembled at the start, Simon Morant wasted no time in setting them on their way, with outsider No Retreat being slow to jump off. In remarkable scenes, and fully aware that this was going to be a race where only the strongest would survive, the field thundered over a completely saturated Melling Road, complete with puddles of water.

It was Edmond who led at the first fence, with the top weight Beau on his outside, and as the leaders flew the fence well, Spanish Main blundered towards the back of the field and unseated Jamie Goldstein on to the heavy, boggy turf. Art Prince found himself on the floor after one jump for the second consecutive year, leaving Pipe with a mere nine runners in the race!

Hanakham, one of two representatives for Donald McCain, came down hard at the second, where both Tresor De Mai and veteran Addington Boy also departed the contest. The big ditch saw three more bow out, including Paddy's Return, who broke Adrian Maguire's one hundred percent completion record in the race. All the money poured onto Inis Cara was soon evaporating into the murky Aintree air as the horse took a spectacular dive at the fourth, and with Earthmover and The Last Fling also eliminated, the field had already lost over a quarter of its runners as they headed for Becher's Brook.

With runners slipping and sliding everywhere in the rain and mud, Beau, Esprit De Cotte, Edmond and Merry People were the leading quartet at Becher's. Although they jumped the fence well, behind them a mistake by the previous year's John Hughes Trophy winner, little Northern Starlight, resulted in the unseating of young amateur Tom Scudamore, son of former champion jockey, Peter. Two more of Martin Pipe's team, Strong Tel and Exit Swinger, had also fallen and a bad mistake saw the end of Merry People a fence later.

Having lost his jockey Maguire at the third, the blinkered Paddy's Return had continued on his way at a strong gallop on the wide outside as he joined the rest of the field approaching the Canal Turn. All of a sudden, as if receiving a signal to detonate a building, the rider-less horse veered violently along the face of the fence. Just avoiding the leading group, and coming within a whisker of colliding with Red Marauder, he proceeded to cause carnage to the rest of the field. With no room to jump, runners either refused or were brought down and, in total, ten horses were put out of the race in the dramatic pile-up, including fancied runners Moral Support and Mely Moss, although Lance Armstrong was able to continue after being remounted.

With chaos in the background, Beau, Edmond and Blowing Wind led on, while Mister One and Esprit De Cotte became the latest casualties out in the country. All this had left just thirteen horses of the forty that started, together with a large bunch of loose horses, to cross the Melling Road with well over a circuit still to run.

If the survivors thought the worst was behind them they were wrong, as the quietly fancied chestnut Noble Lord crashed out at the thirteenth, while at the Chair, Edmond was still right in contention when he appeared to show a dislike for the monster fence and barely took off, resulting in a crushing fall which left the following Brave Highlander to perform some nifty footwork to avoid the fallen market leader. At the same fence, Moondigua and Supreme Charm unseated their riders to leave the field very sparse indeed.

With just seven horses left in an already unbelievable race, the survivors not only had to worry about lasting home on the stamina-sapping ground, but also the vast number of loose horses that were charging around, acting as booby-traps to those still in contention. With each player holding a seemingly equal chance at this point, Beau led Smarty, Blowing Wind, Red Marauder, Papillon, Unsinkable Boxer and Brave Highlander out for another lap.

Red Marauder is almost there after jumping the last in 2001.

The next drama was not long in coming, as Beau made a slight mistake at the seventeenth, leaving Carl Llewellyn with reins on only one side and with barely any control over the horse. Then, at the nineteenth, a loose horse wiped out the challenges of Blowing Wind, Papillon and Brave Highlander, forcing all three to refuse. By the next, Beau, who was still leading and travelling strongly, blundered and unseated Llewellyn. Knowing that he had been denied a great opportunity of another National win, Llewellyn desperately ran after his runaway partner and called out to officials to stop him jumping the next fence so he could be remounted, but his efforts were in vain and his race was unluckily lost. With Unsinkable Boxer pulled up as well, the Grand National of 2001 was now a match between two horses, Smarty and Red Marauder, as they jumped the twenty-first fence.

Sensibly, the two jockeys slowed the pace down and the pair matched strides for a long way. Red Marauder had made a number of mistakes and appeared to be jumping slowly, initially giving Timmy Murphy the edge on Smarty. However, by the time the two weary warriors rounded the turn for home, Richard Guest had pushed his game mount clear and now it was obvious that only a fall would stop Red Marauder winning, as the gallant Smarty had come to the end of his tether in the gruelling conditions.

Despite making an awful hash of the second last, a thoroughly exhausted but incredibly brave Red Marauder saw out the rest of the race to come home a distance clear of Smarty. Immediately, the mud-covered Richard Guest dismounted his shattered partner and gave him an ecstatic hug. With the winner and Smarty the only two to complete the course without incident, Blowing Wind and Papillon were remounted and helped each other to the closing stages of the vicious marathon, before Tony McCoy pulled clear to take third on Blowing Wind, the jockey's first completion in the race.

So, the most dramatic and incident packed Grand National in recent history was won by Red Marauder, whom winning jockey Richard Guest had described as probably the worst jumper ever to win the race. Even if he had not been the safest of conveyances, Red Marauder had displayed the heart of a lion to survive the wretched conditions and claim his place among the National heroes after a race that saw the smallest number of finishers since Tipperary Tim beat the sole other survivor Billy Barton in 1928.

Guest, assistant and stable jockey to winning trainer Norman Mason, had once thrown his jockey's licence at stewards after becoming disillusioned with race decisions that had gone against him, but had now gloriously gone one better in the big race than he did on Romany King back in 1992.

Permit holder Norman Mason was a multi-millionaire businessman and had a team of twenty-one horses – ten with the word 'Red' in them, due to it being a lucky colour for the Chinese nation. Mason was certainly feeling very lucky after Red Marauder's gutsy win, and the trainer graciously gave all the credit to Guest, who he insisted was the heart, soul and driving force behind his stable.

Although the severe state of the ground came in for a lot of criticism, all forty horses returned home safe and sound; it had been proved yet again that the Grand National is a race that is incomparable. The future awaits many more exciting races with brilliant jockeys and courageous horses, the fastest and luckiest of which are destined to write their names into the history books of racing's annual spectacular.

HORSE/FATE	AGE/WEIGHT	JOCKEY	ODDS
1st RED MARAUDER	11.10-11	RICHARD GUEST	33/1
2nd SMARTY	8.10-0	T.J. MURPHY	16/1
3rd BLOWING WIND	8.10-9	A.P. McCOY - *Remount*	16/1
4th PAPILLON	10.11-5	R. WALSH - *Remount*	14/1
Beau - *Unseated Rider*	8.11-10	C. Llewellyn	12/1
Earthmover - *Unseated Rider*	10.11-2	J. Tizzard	22/1
Tresor De Mai - *Fell*	7.11-2	R. Greene	66/1
General Wolfe - *Brought Down*	12.11-0	B.J. Crowley	50/1
The Last Fling - *Unseated Rider*	11.10-12	S. Durack	20/1
Hanakham - *Fell*	12.10-11	B.J. Geraghty	100/1
Addington Boy - *Unseated Rider*	13.10-11	J.P. McNamara	33/1
Djeddah - *Unseated Rider*	10.10-11	T. Doumen	33/1
Strong Tel - *Fell*	11.10-11	D.J. Casey	33/1
Unsinkable Boxer - *Pulled Up*	12.10-10	D. Gallagher	66/1
Moral Support - *Brought Down*	9.10-9	N. Fehily	10/1*
Northern Starlight - *Unseated Rider*	10.10-7	Mr T. Scudamore	50/1
Noble Lord - *Fell*	8.10-5	J.A. McCarthy	25/1
Amberleigh House - *Brought Down*	9.10-5	W. Marston	150/1
Exit Swinger - *Fell*	6.10-5	C. Maude	50/1
Mely Moss - *Brought Down*	10.10-5	N. Williamson	14/1
Dark Stranger - *Refused*	10.10-3	K.A. Kelly	25/1
Listen Timmy - *Pulled Up*	12.10-3	A. Dobbin	100/1
Inis Cara - *Fell*	9.10-3	R. Widger	10/1*
Edmond - *Fell*	9.10-1	R. Johnson	10/1*
You're Agoodun - *Brought Down*	9.10-1	R. Wakley	28/1
No Retreat - *Pulled Up*	8.10-2	J.M. Maguire	100/1
Hollybank Buck - *Fell*	11.10-0	F.J. Flood	20/1
Moondigua - *Unseated Rider*	9.10-0	J.R. Barry	100/1
Village King - *Fell*	8.10-0	J. Culloty	25/1
Spanish Main - *Unseated Rider*	7.10-0	J. Goldstein	25/1
Esprit De Cotte - *Unseated Rider*	9.10-0	T. Doyle	33/1
Lance Armstrong - *Pulled Up*	11.10-2	A. Thornton	50/1
Kaki Crazy - *Fell*	6.10-0	R. Farrant	66/1
Feels Like Gold - *Refused*	13.10-0	B. Harding	50/1
Paddy's Return - *Unseated Rider*	9.10-0	A. Maguire	16/1
Brave Highlander - *Refused*	13.10-0	P. Hide	33/1
Art Prince - *Fell*	11.10-0	J. Crowley	150/1
Mister One - *Unseated Rider*	10.10-0	M. Bradburne	50/1
Supreme Charm - *Unseated Rider*	9.10-0	R. Thornton	33/1
Merry People - *Unseated Rider*	13.10-0	G. Cotter	66/1